IT Solutions Series

Managing Data Mining
Advice from Experts

Stephan Kudyba, Ph.D.
New Jersey Institute of Technology/Null Sigma Inc.,
USA

CYBERTECH Publishing
Hershey • London • Melbourne • Singapore

Senior Managing Editor:	Jan Travers
Managing Editor:	Amanda Appicello
Development Editor:	Michele Rossi
Copy Editor:	Maria Boyer
Typesetter:	Jennifer Wetzel
Cover Design:	Lisa Tosheff
Printed at:	Yurchak Printing Inc.

Published in the United States of America by
CyberTech Publishing (an imprint of Idea Group Inc.)
701 E. Chocolate Avenue, Suite 200
Hershey PA 17033 USA
Tel: 717-533-8845
Fax: 717-533-8661
E-mail: cust@idea-group.com
Web site: http://www.idea-group.com

and in the United Kingdom by
CyberTech Publishing (an imprint of Idea Group Inc.)
3 Henrietta Street
Covent Garden
London WC2E 8LU
Tel: 44 20 7240 0856
Fax: 44 20 7379 3313
Web site: http://www.eurospan.co.uk

Library of Congress Cataloging-in-Publication Data

Managing data mining : advice from experts / Stephan Kudyba, editor.
       p. cm. -- (IT solutions series)
    Includes bibliographical references and index.
     ISBN 1-59140-243-3 (pbk.)
  1. Data mining. I. Kudyba, Stephan, 1963- II. Series.
    QA76.9.D343M36 2004
    006.3'12--dc22
                                                                    2004003688

British Cataloguing in Publication Data
A Cataloguing in Publication record for this book is available from the British Library.

IT Solutions Series:

Managing Data Mining
Advice from Experts

Foreword

Dr. Jim Goodnight
CEO & President, SAS

In response to increasingly high customer demands and formidable competition, today's organizations have implemented new technologies that generate and collect massive volumes of data. However, a large majority of the data collected goes to waste or becomes obsolete. Inconsistency, repetition, time-sensitivity, disparate data sources and data overkill are just a few of the problems overwhelming many decision makers.

Fortunately, the need for digestible and useful data has created a new generation of business intelligence technologies. This includes software that sifts through mountain ranges of data until the most useful nuggets of information are extracted and identified, much the same way that California prospectors of the 19th century refined their techniques to strike gold more quickly.

This new technology, commonly known as *Data Mining,* has taken on a life of its own and continues to evolve.

Data Mining is the science of revealing useful patterns and relationships in vast data stores. Data Mining — considered by many as the new name for statistics — draws on many disciplines. With statistics as its foundation, it incorporates computer science, machine learning, artificial intelligence and other specialties. Data Mining ultimately provides a framework for dealing with uncertainty. As organizations and the global economy become more complex, sources of uncertainty become more plentiful. To make decisions confidently, new and sophisticated approaches are required.

The vast quantities of data that businesses produce, gather and store fuel the demand for more effective means of deriving value from them. Technologies that distill value from data have been available for some time. We have long been able to ask simple questions of the data: What were sales last quarter? How did the western region do compared to the eastern region? This book is not about such query and reporting or OLAP. These tools, while necessary, do not generate the big returns, nor do they provide answers to the really challenging questions. Business managers have often shied away from high-end data analysis, perhaps fearing it to be overly complex. With ever-increasing quantities of data, and lots of questions needing better answers, a growing number of decision makers want to know what Data Mining can do for them.

Today's powerful multivariate modeling techniques provide answers to the hard questions: Which patterns and relationships are truly significant and which are merely chance? What are the really important factors affecting quality and sales? Which customers are likely to leave? Why and when? Given the probabilities of default, what is the exposure for a given portfolio of loans? Analytical rigor is required to effectively address the wide range of growing business needs, such as assessing risk more accurately, improving price optimization, and anticipating customer demand and preferences. Such applications of Data Mining are increasingly possible — and valuable — in business, as the examples in this book clearly demonstrate.

Data Mining delivers on the promise of helping executives make, save and spend money more effectively. Enlightened decision makers now enjoy new peace of mind. They can chart their courses more strategically and with greater precision over longer periods, rather than simply reacting, in fire-drill fashion, to either tactical or strategic issues that flare up. Savvy executives harness the power of Data Mining in new areas of business for superior performance and sustained competitive advantage. No longer is high-end data analysis considered a rare, specialized activity with limited use in business. Instead, corporate survival depends on how well Data Mining is applied to vast and growing data stores.

Data Mining has led to highly refined processes, especially where the stakes are high. Minimizing the downside often piques management's interest first — reducing write-offs, losses and fraud — since these improvements are typically easy to measure. Significant returns can also come from the upside where the potential may be less obvious — increasing customer response, sales and market share. Success breeds success, and the interest in high-end data analysis continues to grow. Only high-end data analysis keeps delivering big returns across increasing areas of business; ROI in excess of 1,000% is not uncommon. Data Mining has become integral to many aspects of business with returns that are significant, yet often incalculable.

In today's data-driven economy, Data Mining is an essential tool in the pursuit of enhanced productivity, reduced uncertainty, delighted customers, mitigated risk, maximized returns, refined processes and optimally allocated resources. To thrive, performance must be measured along the way so that the factors that contributed to success — or failure — can be understood. By applying a more scientific approach to business decision making, the stage is set for continuous learning and improvement.

This book highlights the value of making sound decisions in the face of uncertainty. Real-world examples span industry sectors and illustrate how Data Mining drives optimal decision making for a variety of business processes. The business leaders and experts contributing to this book provide unique insights on a variety of business processes, challenges, solutions and best practices. As Data Mining becomes more ubiquitous in business, let this book serve as an invitation to reap the benefits for those who have not yet begun. And for those who have already embarked, may this book allow greater success.

Dr. James H. Goodnight is CEO, chairman, co-founder and president of SAS Institute, the world's largest privately held software company. Chief executive since the company's incorporation in 1976, Goodnight continues to focus on strategic planning for the global business, which provides software and services that enable customers to transform data from all areas of their business into intelligence. An accomplished programmer, Goodnight has authored many of the procedures that comprise SAS® software.

SAS passed the $1 billion revenue mark in 1999 and revenues continue to grow. According to Goodnight, the key to the company's success has been its ability to listen to more than 3.5 million software users and respond to their needs. SAS customers represent numerous industries and can be found in more than 100 countries. More than 200 SAS offices around the globe support this large customer base. SAS responds to customer needs by staying near the top of the software industry in the percentage of revenue reinvested in research and development, devoting over a quarter of total revenue to R&D.

In addition to this significant investment in technology, Goodnight also invests in people — SAS employees and their families. The company's work environment is designed to nurture and encourage creativity, innovation and quality. Since the early 1980s, Goodnight has supported on-site child care, health care and recreation and fitness centers. His commitment to these progressive work-life programs has earned SAS national recognition in publications such as The Wall Street Journal as well as Fortune, Fast Company, Business Week *and* Working Mother *magazines.*

Goodnight's passion, and the focus of SAS' philanthropic efforts, is education. In August 1997, the doors opened at Cary Academy, an independent college preparatory day school for students in grades 6 through 12. Goodnight co-founded the school in 1996 as a model school — one that integrates technology into all facets of education. Shortly after Cary Academy opened, SAS launched SAS inSchool, which develops content-based educational software that is helping move schools into the next millennium. The software contains the framework for a new generation of teaching courseware that will further the use of technology as a learning tool.

A native of Wilmington, N.C., Goodnight holds bachelor's and master's degrees as well as a doctorate in statistics from North Carolina State University. He served on the faculty of NCSU from 1972 to 1976, and continues to serve as an adjunct professor. Goodnight is a Fellow of the American Statistical Association, and has authored numerous papers on statistical computing.

Preface

The term Data Mining continues to be an elusive concept to many business managers as it is often imbedded in the idea of searching through vast amounts of data records that reside in organizations across industry sectors. The purpose of this book is to help reduce the uncertainty as to what Data Mining really is and more importantly, illustrate how prominent organizations incorporate it in order to enhance their operational efficiency. Without going into great detail at this stage, Data Mining can help augment operational efficiency or enable decision makers to better manage business processes by empowering users to gain a greater understanding of the critical factors that drive corresponding operational activities. Through the combination of data, data management, business modeling and finally applying mining methodologies such as logit regression, segmentation or neural networks, managers can identify not only which variables impact such operational measures such as Sales, Customer Response Rates, Default Propensities but also estimate a quantifiable connection between them. The resulting models provide decision makers with ability to perform "what if" simulations or simply forecast into the future.

Data Mining is not limited to just a few prominent business applications but can provide a value add to a variety of operational activities of organizations across industry sectors. The information in the following chapters will provide a much clearer understanding of some prominent business processes in which it can be utilized as a strategic component to enhancing productivity. More specifically, Chapter I provides a more detailed description of what Data Mining is, what is entailed in conducting a robust mining analysis, why mining has become so much more popular over the past decade, what are some prevalent business processes that mining is utilized and how Data Mining complements and augments existing strategic initiatives such as Six Sigma.

Chapter II entails our first detailed analysis of a prominent business process as it addresses how mining and multivariate modeling can help augment the decision making process in the world of finance, more specifically, how decision makers can better manage the risk associated with lending activities. The chapter was written by two modeling experts from Citigroup who describe the activities entailed in generating multivariate models to help measure risk of both corporate and consumer borrowers. This high level concept is addressed in more detail in Chapter III, where a leading Data Mining consultant describes the process by which quantitative modeling techniques are used to help manage risk in lending to small businesses. The section provides an overview of the lending industry, inherent risks that are involved in it and the types of models (Credit Scoring, New Application Scoring and Behavior Scoring) that can reduce risk. It ends with a small case study which helps drive home the concepts highlighted in the section.

The book then turns its focus towards the realm of Customer Relationship Management, initially in the Insurance industry. Chapter IV is written by a senior business strategist at Chubb Insurance. This section describes key concepts that are involved in applying analytics to better understand customer behavior and preferences and how to best make a connection with them through effectively managing the sales force. Through the effective incorporation of Data, Data Mining & BI, along with sound management policies, organizations can better understand the various needs that correspond to particular consumer groups and with this information, can better direct sales force initiatives in order to make a clearer connection with them. Chapter V extends the description of sales force management but takes a more detailed look at the characteristics of sales representatives. An expert consultant in the field of Data Mining provides a thorough illustration of how to utilize detailed data that describe the activities of sales representatives along with leading quantitative techniques in order to better identify the type of sales reps that are likely to perform well in selling a company's products or services.

Chapter VI diverges from sales force applications but continues to address Customer Relationship Management and organizational operating efficiency. Two experts from one of the largest Health Insurance companies (Blue Cross Blue Shield) describe the process by which firms can incorporate Data Mining and the "high-level" strategic methodology of Six Sigma to help manage product and service costs and corresponding prices in a rising cost industry. Chapter VII continues to focus on the Health Care industry and Customer Relationship Management but concentrates on a different type of business application and consumer. A group of Health Care experts from American Healthways Corp. describe the process by which decision makers can utilize the power of Data Mining to enhance the process of managing potential diseases/illnesses that exist in patients. With this information, health care providers can better allocate resources to reduce potential development of chronic illnesses and better manage overall operational costs.

Chapter VIII takes on a whole new focus as it addresses the world of advertising. A senior partner of a subsidiary of one of the worlds largest advertising organizations (Omnicom Group Inc.) offers some expert insights on how Data Mining and Econometric modeling can better estimate the returns to different strategic initiatives involved in the advertising industry. These include such topics as promotional effectiveness, medium effectiveness and brand awareness. We all know that an organization can have one of the best products on the market, but if no one is aware of it, its sales may suffer. Our next chapter extends the analysis of advertising but shifts towards the world of e-commerce. An expert analyst at Nielsen's//NetRatings provides some background on the Internet marketplace and then addresses such topics as online audience measurement, tracking advertising activities and then describes a model of analyzing consumer online activities. The section then provides a few case studies to drive home concepts more clearly.

Our last chapter delves into the complex task of managing operational risk in an evolving and volatile industry. The recently deregulated Utilities industry, which involves the process of supplying power to a variety of consumers, many times incorporates sophisticated quantitative methods in order to help mitigate the uncertainty in allocating enough power to the marketplace. An expert from Con Edison provides some insightful background information describing the evolution of the industry and then illustrates how decision makers can use quantitative techniques to better manage such variables as price, supply and demand of electricity over various time horizons. This last chapter concludes the content for "Data Mining: Advice from Experts" but highlights an important point to remember regarding the utilization and power of Data Mining techniques, and that is, the quantitative (mathematical and algorithmic) methodologies that comprise this analytic space can be applied to a variety of business applications. Through the use of Data Mining, decision makers can help reduce the uncertainty as to what drives particular business processes and, with this enhanced knowledge, can more efficiently allocate available resources to bring a good or service to market.

Chapter I

Data Mining and the World of Commerce

Stephan Kudyba, PhD
New Jersey Institute of Technology/Null Sigma Inc.,
USA

Introduction

Despite the research written, the software developed and the business applications that can be enhanced by it, the terms *data mining* and *multivariate modeling* continue to stoke uncertainty, complexity and sometimes fear in business managers and strategic decision-makers across industry sectors. Why is this? There are a number of reasons to cite, but probably the most common involves the complex nature of the methodologies incorporated in this analytic technique. The complexity we refer to involves the use of mathematical equations, sophisticated algorithms and advanced search and query techniques, not to mention statistical applications that are utilized in analyzing data. If that is not enough to throw management back on their heels, how about data acquisition, normalization, and model optimization, which are often involved in the process? Let's add one more attribute to the list, and that is the ability to not only understand these complex methods, but more importantly, to understand when and where they can be used to enhance operational efficiency. Now is there any wonder why data mining continues to be this mysterious phenomenon in the world of commerce? No doubt; however, to dispel some of the uncertainties regarding this issue, the following book will provide the reader with expert input on how these quantitative methods are being used in prominent organizations in a variety of industry sectors to help enhance productivity, efficiency and to some extent, profitability. Before we get into the details of the applied material, the following chapter will provide some general information on what data mining and multivariate modeling is, where it came from, and how it can be used in a corporate setting to enhance operational efficiency.

Data Mining and Multivariate Modeling (What Is It?)

Before we begin a book entitled *IT Solutions: Data Mining, Advice from Experts*, we will need to provide some basic background of what the term *data mining* refers to. Without committing to a formal definition, let's initially focus on the big picture. In order to do this we need to begin with the first term, data, a word that should not be underestimated. Given the evolution of the Information Economy, where innovations in information technology have facilitated the ability to store, manipulate, organize and generally process data, organizations have increasingly become aware of the valuable information that is available to them. Data exist both within a given organization (e.g., operational, customer activity based) and also outside the boundaries of corporate entities (e.g., industry and market specific descriptive data). By combining elements of these resources and analyzing data variables with appropriate methodologies, companies can increase their understanding of how effectively their strategic initiatives perform in the market in which they operate.

This previous sentence, which mentions "analyzing with appropriate methodologies", provides a logical lead into the overall terms of data mining and multivariate modeling. These concepts involve the processing of data that have been collected, normalized, corrected and organized, which incorporate key variables that describe the essential underpinnings of a business process. Processing generally refers to the application of mathematical equations or algorithms, sometimes in conjunction with statistical verification techniques that help identify relationships between these variables. Prominent data mining and multivariate modeling techniques include:

- Regression
- Logistic Regression
- Clustering
- Segmentation Classification
- Neural Networks
- Affinity Analysis

The quantitative and statistical techniques incorporated in these methodologies help identify reliable relationships that may exist between the variables that describe a business process. With this information, managers increase their understanding of how certain variables generally relate to each other in describing a business process, and the resulting models also empower them to perform simulations (e.g., "what-ifs") to gain a greater understanding of future expectations of business performance measures given a set of strategic variable inputs.

Business Intelligence Technology
(A Complement to Data Mining)

A complementary data processing activity to the data mining spectrum involves the activity of querying databases and organizing data variables into report form or into cubes of information that can be analyzed in a basic context. OLAP (Online Analytic Processing) provides users with the ability to view variables that describe a business process and perform data manipulation to view variables according to different formats in a numeric and graphical context. OLAP cubes give users a preliminary look at what drives particular business processes across an organization, as it presents a multi-dimensional view of the various factors that explain a process. What do we mean by a multidimensional view? Well, we can almost compare the term "multidimensional" with "multivariate", mentioned above. Simply put, multidimensional refers to the variety of characteristics or variables that describe/explain the operational activities of an organization.

For example, if you are a sales executive and wish to gain a greater understanding of your sales activities over the past year, you could access an OLAP-based "sales cube". This cube of information gives the user the ability to analyze sales performance measures such as sales/revenue, unit sales, profit metrics, and so forth, corresponding to descriptive variables of their sales activities such as particular products or product lines in a particular region (East Coast) over a particular time period (quarterly, monthly), in which each variable mentioned is a dimension. The cube enables users to quickly change dimensions of the analysis with just a click of a mouse (see Figure 1).

Figure 1

Time	Product Line	Region	Outlet	Measure
Quarterly	Sporting	NY City	Retail	Units Sold

2002	Golf Clubs	Golf Bags	Golf Shoes
Qrtr1	25,000	5,200	2,230
Qrtr2	27,000	5,340	2,450
Qrtr3	15,000	4,000	1,760
Qrtr4	19,200	4,760	1,980

The process of creating a cube from data in a data warehouse or mart to enable users to analyze a particular operational activity of a firm is a major technological component of the business intelligence spectrum and is addressed in a number of chapters throughout this book.

Growing Utilization of Data Mining

Despite the power complementary business intelligence methodologies such as OLAP provide for business users, analysts and managers at all levels often need to go beyond gaining a greater understanding of what their operational activities have looked like in the past. They need to answer more complex questions such as, "What can I expect in the future if I take specific strategic actions?" As we mentioned, because of the mathematical and quantitative techniques incorporated by data mining, users can build models that can help them answer these "what if" scenarios. But when considering the more prominent reasons behind the increase in popularity and utilization of data mining over the past few years, one needs to turn to some factors that are related to the general evolution of the information economy.

Some of the prominent reasons why data mining has become a common strategic tool of corporations across industry sectors include such areas as:

- Enhancements in computer processing and increased ease of use of data mining software technology.

- The ability to capture and store data that describe the operational activities of organizations.

- The pulse of business process management which entails strategic utilization of available resources to enhance operational efficiency.

Enhancements in Technology

Let's take a more detailed look at what we mean by enhancements in computer processing capabilities. We only need to go back less than a decade to note the introduction of Pentium processing to the world of mainframe and laptop computers. This increased processing capability significantly enhanced a computer's ability to process larger amounts of data. It also provided the platform for the development of a host of innovative software applications that enhanced the general usability of hardware technology. As innovations in processing, hardware storage and software applications continued with the evolution of the information economy, so too did the ability to store, manipulate, process, analyze and communicate data and information in the world of commerce.

Data: A Vital Resource

This last concept introduces another major component that has led to the increased use of data mining methodologies, and this refers to the word "data". The data explosion that began in the mid-1990s has gained significant momentum. Why? Not just because companies have a greater ability to store data, but more importantly, because data are a vital resource of essential information that can provide greater clarity as to the factors that drive the functional activities of an organization. Data can hold the key to describing why particular strategic initiatives were successful or unsuccessful. As a result, organizations have continued to expand their activities in acquiring, storing and analyzing data, both internal to their company and from external sources that provide information about the marketplace in which they operate. What we are referring to is the analysis of data sources from internal data warehouses and marts that contain information about the operational activities of the organization, and data from external sources such as Dunn and Bradstreet and Lexus Nexus that provide information about competitors and the general industry in which a firm operates.

Data Management

The concept of data and information, however, is not as simple as it appears. In order to effectively extract the productive resource data can provide, organizations must undertake painful procedures in data management and data transformation. What are some of these painful procedures? Well, let's start with a seemingly simple but incredibly complex task to manage from a company perspective, and this addresses the question of, "What data should an organization capture?" In other words, what variables and at what level of detail does a firm store data in a data repository in order for them to better understand their functional activities in the realm of the market in which they operate? Now let's bring this concept to a whole new dimension by considering it in the context of a Fortune 100 firm that operates around the globe and is involved in the production, distribution and ultimate retail of its goods and services to diverse consumer markets in a variety of countries both via a brick and mortar and e-commerce platforms.

Before we try to respond to this perplexing task, let's just consider the concept of data storage and data warehousing. Organizations must effectively manage the processes of:

- Identifying the type of data (e.g., what variables) that help them better understand their operational activities.
- Determine the level of detail in which these data must be collected (e.g., at the transactional level).
- Determine the frequency with which these data are collected (e.g., at the point of sale on a minute-by-minute basis through Electronic Data Interchange).

Once these essential elements have been determined, the data management process then incorporates another essential and complex facet and this involves the mechanism in which data are stored. More specifically:

- Does an organization establish one central repository (warehouse)?
- Does it incorporate a more focused level of data storage by constructing data marts?

The process unfortunately does not end there. The data storage facility must be effectively managed to promote easy data access, data identification, and new data input, to name a few. To accomplish this, data must be organized in relational structures, sometimes incorporating star schema platforms that involve well designed metadata identification mechanisms. Addressing the concept of developing optimal data management procedures is beyond the scope of this book, as our focus is more to extract the productivity enhancing resource that data can provide with the use of data mining techniques. So in order to connect the worlds of data storage, data management and data mining, we will introduce a timely and popular "buzz-phrase" referred to as Business Process Management (BPM).

Business Process Management

What is BPM and is there any validity to it? Business process management refers to the initiative of applying appropriate management strategy, incorporating all available productive resources, to increase the efficiency or productivity of a particular operational activity. Resources refer to the traditional organizational inputs such as labor, technology and materials. Business process management has become increasingly popular as new information technologies (software, hardware, telecomm) have enabled managers to retool existing functional activities with the goal of increasing overall efficiency. The application of data mining techniques helps decision-makers uncover important relationships among data variables that describe a particular business process. Ultimately, with a better understanding of what drives a process, decision-makers can adjust available resources (e.g., labor, technology, materials) to enhance the efficiency in which they are carried out. Some common business processes include:

- Production and Manufacturing
- Distribution
- Sales
- Marketing
- Customer Service

More complex processes incorporate a combination of the traditional elements mentioned with a more strategic focus. These include:

- Customer Relationship Management
- Supply Chain Management
- Human Resource Management

The above processes are often further broken down by sub-functions such as:

- Sales Force Management
- Call Center Management
- Material and Shipment Management

So how does Business process management integrate the concepts of data storage, data management and data mining? In order to achieve a greater understanding of what drives a particular business process, decision-makers must create models that contain the data and information that describe a process. These data-based business models can ultimately take the form of an advanced Excel spreadsheet or an OLAP cube to perform static analysis of business activities or can be created by applying various data mining techniques to selected data that establish the quantitative connection between explanatory variables and a given performance variable. The business model creation process therefore requires decision-makers to determine the types of variables that describe a particular business process: (variable format and degree of aggregation).

Driving Operational Efficiency Through Data Mining and BPM

Taking the next step to actually achieving increased operational efficiency for a given organization incorporates the combination of available data, input from experienced management, and key insights in business activities that are identified by data mining. As was mentioned above, almost every organization in most any type of industry sector performs a variety of operational activities in order to bring a product or service to market. The key to carrying out these activities more efficiently (e.g., through better resource allocation) requires that decision-makers more fully understand what makes these processes tick, both internally to the corresponding firm, and of course, externally with competitors and the general market in which they operate. One essential way to achieve an increased understanding of strategic initiatives and operational activities is through the analysis of the data that describe them, and one of the most effective ways of analyzing data is through data mining. Let's take a few prominent business processes to drive this topic home.

Marketing and Promotional Campaigns

Whether it is direct mail campaigns or the use of various mediums of advertising (e.g., print, TV), organizations allocate a substantial sum of money to promote a given product or service to the market. The key to driving operational efficiency and even profitability with regards to these business processes requires that decision-makers fine-tune their corresponding resource alloca-tions. What does this mean? In reference to direct mail marketing, decision-makers can increase their efficiency through simply better identifying consumers that are likely to respond positively to the campaign. By doing so, the firm can enhance their performance by:

1. Reducing the amount of mailings while maintaining the same number of positive responses or
2. Increasing the number of positive responses with the original amount of mailings.

The result of the first tactic is a reduction in marketing costs, while the second is an increase in overall product sales through the increased number of positive responses.

Data mining can drive this increased efficiency by enabling decision-makers to better identify:

• The type of consumer that is likely to respond to particular marketing initiatives.

• The type of consumer that is likely to consume more (e.g., spend more on your products and services).
• The type of marketing or promotional campaign that is most effective for a given product or service line.

The bottom line to the strategic initiative of utilizing data mining is to enable users to identify previously unknown relationships between variables that describe a particular process (e.g., con-sumer demographics and likelihood to respond to a marketing initiative in the example), which increases their understanding as to what drives the process, both internal to the firm and external in the marketplace. This increased understanding is a reduction in uncertainty in the effective allocation of available resources that drive an operational or business process. Some prominent relationships that data mining techniques can uncover in data, which ultimately can better explain what drives a particular business process, include:

Demographic and behavioral data (B2B or B2C) on:
1. Likelihood to default on a loan
2. Likelihood to purchase
3. Likelihood to commit fraud
4. Likelihood to respond to a cross or up-sell
5. Likelihood to cancel a policy...
    ...and many more.

Other examples of relationships that data mining can help identify between input variables and corresponding performance variables of a business process can include:

Input/Driver Variable	Performance Variable
• Price of a (Product/Service)	Sales Revenue of (Product/Service)
• Advertising Expenditure	Product Sales or Market Share
• Call Center Activities	Consumer Satisfaction Rate
• Motivational Tactics & Demographic Characteristics	Employee Performance
• Behavioral & Descriptive Attributes of Suppliers	Production Quality and Product Time to Market
• Descriptive Attributes of Retail Stores and Geographic Store Locations	Retail Store Sales
...and many more	

Closing Points on Data Mining and Corporate Productivity (Six Sigma)

You have probably heard the term Six Sigma used around your company in various settings in reference to a variety of issues. Without going into any great detail behind this philosophy, the following section will provide a simple connection on how data mining can be a complementary strategic tool in driving Six Sigma results.

Organizations such as GE and Motorola are widely cited as some of the early initiators of implementing the Six Sigma philosophy into the operational activities of their organizations, and early efforts largely addressed manufacturing and production processes. Today, however, companies are using this approach to help improve their efficiency in a variety of processes, from marketing to customer support. Corporations are now utilizing a vital resource called "data" that describes their operational activities to fine-tune strategic initiatives. Does this sound familiar? Before we go any further, let's clarify what we mean by Six Sigma and corporate productivity. Generally, Six Sigma seeks to reduce the uncertainty in the variability of various operational outcomes. In other words, decision-makers seek to reduce the amount of product defects in a particular production batch (e.g., traditional Six Sigma). Today they seek to enhance the response rate for a particular marketing initiative, increase client call resolution rates for a particular number of agents at a call center, reduce the amount of product stockouts at a particular retail outlet, and increase cross-sell rates per customer contact.

Six Sigma largely incorporates quantitative and statistical methods to analyze data in order to better detect flaws, defects, unacceptable variances and relationships among variables that describe a business process. It is this quantitative approach by which data mining can play a role in helping achieve Six Sigma. By incorporating mathematical and statistical approaches, data mining methodologies help decision-makers better identify the potential causes behind variances in operational output variables such as product defects and customer satisfaction rates, and through more effective resource allocation, can ultimately reduce output variances and enhance operational performance.

Not a One-Time Procedure

As is the case with any strategic initiative seeking to enhance corporate efficiency, data mining analysis requires a continuous process that needs to be managed. Earlier in this chapter we addressed the steps that are essential to conducting a value added analysis through data mining (e.g., data management, business expert input, identifying a business process to improve); however, the mining/modeling process is not a one-time project. Data mining analysis leads strategic decision-makers to take action in order to increase efficiency, productivity and profitability. These initiatives need to be monitored to determine whether the corresponding plans of action accomplished what they set out to do. In other words...

- Did your organization increase the amount of responses for a given marketing campaign?
- Did your company's cross-sell rate improve?
- Did your sales force close more deals?
- Did you reduce your loan losses?

There are generally two answers to the questions above. Either your processes have become more efficient or they have not. Either response requires decision-makers to work with the situation at hand. If your process has improved, you need to understand the factors that drove the success and build on them. If they have not improved, you need to identify why. When considering these issues in context of data mining, you may want to ask some simple questions.

- Was your mining analysis inaccurate (and if so, why)?
- Did you miss important variables in your business process?
- Is your market more dynamic than initially estimated (e.g., are your competitors outsmarting you)?

In order to consistently achieve enhanced operating efficiency, decision-makers must continuously use the tools and information available to better understand the market in which they participate.

What to Expect From This Book

This chapter has provided a high level view as to what the world of data mining and corporate productivity entails. This included some basic background as to what data mining is and the prominent methodologies that comprise this quantitative analytic concept. We then provided some essential information on the issue of data management, which generally stresses the notion that the word "data" in data mining should not be taken lightly. Finally we connected the value add that data mining provides to the world of commerce, which is the primary reason why we put this book together. By reading this chapter you should therefore gain greater insights from the material offered in the coming chapters.

The following information in this book was written by business leaders and data mining experts that operate in a variety of industries and manage a variety of business processes.

Some of the topics and business applications that you will encounter include:

- Sales Force Efficiency
- Customer Relationship Management
- Credit Risk and General Risk Management
- Advertising and Marketing Effectiveness
- E-commerce Strategic Analysis
- Healthcare Management

The authors of corresponding chapters provide insightful content on how data mining is used in these prominent business applications at some of the largest organizations in the world. The information is presented by a general descriptive approach, graphic illustrations and case studies and incorporates many of the concepts that have been introduced to you in this first chapter. Through this approach we attempt to provide a clearer picture of how strategic decision-makers can use powerful tools such as data mining and multivariate modeling to improve their resource allocation in order to increase their efficiency, productivity and ultimately, profitability.

The following chapter will address the topic of managing risk in lending practices in the financial services sector through the utilization of data mining and multivariate modeling techniques. It will cover lending practices to both corporate entities and the private consumer.

Chapter II

Data Mining and the Banking Sector:
Managing Risk in Lending and Credit Card Activities

Àkos Felsõvályi and Jennifer Courant
Citigroup, USA

Introduction

Banking has changed rapidly over the last decades due to the ability to capture massive data sets easily and the availability of new tools for analysis. The new, commonly used expressions to describe these phenomena are data warehousing and data mining.

The changes have transformed traditional banking activities such as extending loans and given birth to new businesses. For example, the credit card business would simply not exist today, or not in today's form, without the use of high powered computers and new statistical methods.

In this chapter, we will discuss a few areas of this vast and important phenomenon, following the outline presented. We will be focusing on corporate lending, although data mining permeates all aspects of today's banking. Some aspects of the corporate lending discussion are based on Citigroup's own practices, and the rest of the subject will be based on practices generic to the industry.

The chapter outline is as follows:

1. Traditional Lending
    1.1 Corporate Lending
    1.2 Consumer Lending
2. Credit Card Activities

Traditional Lending and Corporations

Introduction to Risk Assessment

One of the key areas in banking is corporate lending, in which a bank loans money to a company for a set period of time at a given interest rate. The decision to make a loan is not easy. All companies are exposed to various situations, such as rising and falling interest rates, economic/business cycles, industry cycles, and so forth, which will affect the likelihood that the company may not repay the loan at the agreed upon terms. Traditionally, banks have focused their analysis on assessing this risk of non-repayment — or default — on the loan. Increasingly, however, banks are realizing (and trying to measure) a second, yet equally important part of the credit risk that the bank takes on when lending to a variety of obligors — the losses incurred if there is a default.

The importance of measuring and understanding credit risk — both the likelihood of default and loss incurred if there is a default — is vital to the banks' decision-making processes. Credit risk factors into a variety of aspects of the banks' business, such as how they identify their risk appetite and choose their customer base, how they market different loan products to different customers and, finally, how they price loans. The better a bank is at identifying and assessing the credit risks it takes on from its lending activities, the better it can maximize its return on those risks taken. The ideal situation is not necessarily for the bank to identify all possible customers that are the least risky and only do business with those customers. It could, instead, choose to identify the risk profile it would like to maintain as best as possible. Once identified, the bank would strive to price products according to the risk taken on each customer and thereby maximize the return given the risk taken. By assessing and pricing for the risk appropriately, banks can, theoretically, widen their target markets to encompass a broader risk spectrum.

Predicting the risk profile, or default likelihood, of a prospective customer is difficult, as we are predicting an event — default — with a low probability of occurring. Even in 2001 and 2002, when there were a record numbers of defaults, the overall risk of default among corporations is a rare event.

Not identifying a defaulting or deteriorating company, or "getting it wrong", has a high penalty for the bank in terms of credit losses. For example, lending in Argentina or to Kmart recently resulted in severe credit losses for many institutions. One can also recall Bank of New England's foray into real estate lending, which contributed to that bank's insolvency in January 1991. Identifying a company that does not default as a likely defaulter (a "false positive") also translates into a costly proposition, because there is a loss of business and opportunity. As a result, there is a strong incentive to "get it right": that is, to accurately identify companies that will default, while minimizing the mistaken identification of non-defaulters as companies likely to default. There is no benefit in erring on the conservative side, since business opportunities may be lost to institutions that are more accurate in assessing credit risk.

Rather, there is always a benefit in trying to minimize any errors on both sides. The key here is the collection of data and utilizing those data to create models that will help identify companies with weak or declining credit worthiness.

Finally, success in risk management is a difficult and time consuming concept to measure. The relationship a bank has with its customers is not a second-by-second relationship. It is a relationship that is built over time and it takes observation and data collection over the lifetime of a loan in order to determine whether the prediction of default or deterioration was accurate.

Risk Assessment Today

Data Warehousing and Credit Risk Modeling

Prior to the real estate collapse and leveraged buyouts of the late 1980s and the economic recession of the early 1990s, very little statistically based risk assessment was done. Most banks, and other arbiters of risk analysis (including rating agencies Moody's and Standard and Poor's) relied on the expert opinion of loan officers, credit officers and analysts, rather than any objective, statistical analysis.

After the crisis, banks became interested in how they could understand and manage the credit risk they were taking as part of their business on a more consistent basis. For example, Citigroup began an initiative to warehouse data that would be used to assist in risk assessment and utilize new data mining methods to analyze them. This effort involves the collection, storage and maintenance of large amounts of data, application of advanced modeling techniques, and constant monitoring and validation of the models that are in use.

A wide variety of data are necessary to analyze credit risk. Information on a company's financial position is one of the key pieces of this necessary data, which is generally acquired via its annual financial statements. In the United States, for instance, financial statement data are readily available for companies that trade on one of the exchanges, as they are required to submit financial statements in a timely fashion to the Securities and Exchange Commission (SEC). An interested party can buy large data sets of company financials from a vendor or download statements from the SEC's EDGAR website.

A side note to warehousing data and modeling in the United States is that approximately 1,800 public U.S. companies are rated by one of the public rating agencies. For some institutions, ratings available from the agencies have mitigated the need for internal credit risk models, although larger institutions clearly need better coverage of companies that are not rated. There are clear risks to sole reliance on agency ratings. Since 2001, there has been a record number of "fallen angels" documented by the agencies. A fallen angel is a company rated investment grade that is downgraded to non-investment grade (or "junk" status). In some cases, the deterioration may have, in fact, been quite sudden. In others, it was clear that the agencies resisted downgrading the companies until the brink of default. While the key rating agencies have publicly committed to more timely downgrades, they are also concerned about volatile ratings, and some would charge, have a conflict of interest in rating companies that pay for those ratings.

Moving outside the United States, data are not as easy to buy and timely reporting requirements are not necessarily as stringent. Because Citigroup has been doing business in over 100 countries on all continents (excluding Antarctica) for many years, we have access to both data and expertise across a wide population of corporations. As such, Citigroup requires effective credit assessment tools that produce ratings that are not only accurate but globally consistent.

Regardless of where a company is domiciled, a key aspect of data collection behind the development of credit tools focuses on defaulted companies: both the identification of "default" and also collection of financial information prior to default on this set of companies. Building a warehouse of financial statements of defaulted companies, with statements at least one year prior to default, is essential if we are to build models to predict the one year probability of default (which is an accepted time horizon in risk assessment). In effect, the only means of "validating" a model's accuracy against defaults is to be able to test it against actual defaults. If we can actively test the models against current or recent defaulted companies, we can make a judgment about the quality of the model today. A true benefit for credit risk modeling at Citigroup is that we have more than 30 years of history on internal defaults across all businesses and regions. Those internal data, combined with research into non-customer defaults to build a global default database, have greatly enhanced our credit risk modeling efforts and allowed us to move toward models that directly measure default, rather than a rating category.

Internally, we also have access to a wealth of history on nonfinancial characteristics of companies, as well as industry segmentation. Generally, industrial data are gathered from outside vendors, as well as internal sources. Industrial data include general data on the industries with which we are working and information about a particular company's position relative to its peers in the industry. The existence of models and a rating-based credit process for more than 13 years at Citigroup has allowed us to collect a variety of data regarding a company's market position, management quality, the risk appetite of management, quality of audited statements, time in business and time as a customer.

The next critical phase after data collection is data cleaning. No matter how much data we have, inconsistencies or inaccuracies can seriously jeopardize the quality of any modeling effort. Data quality is a concern whether we are working with our own internal data or data from a vendor and unlike market data, credit risk data (such as financial statements) are "low frequency" (annual data in most instances). As such, almost every data point is valuable and serious effort is made to ensure that the data are accurate, while we discard as little data as possible. Many elements of the data will be checked, both through automated and manual processes. For instance, does the balance sheet balance, does the income statement flow properly to the reported net income, and can we confirm the default date?

Finally, this large warehouse of data, both customer and non-customer, which spans many years and many countries, will be used in modeling different aspects of credit risk that the bank will utilize in assessing the credit quality of a client.

Various Models of Risk Assessment

Basic Models to Measure Credit Risk

As a starting point, lenders need basic credit risk calculators to assess the credit worthiness of their customers. At Citigroup, those calculators are called Credit Risk Models. The large amount of financial and ratings data that the bank has actively collected and accumulated over the last 13 years, along with the extensive default database, allow researchers to build a variety of models that measure credit risk and associate that risk with a given probability of default. In line with the rating agencies, the bank utilizes a 10-

category rating system with notching around each category (similar to S&P's system of letters such as AA+, AA, AA-, etc.). Unlike the agency ratings, each category is associated with a range of probabilities of default at Citigroup. There are models covering Citigroup's commercial and industrial customers (i.e., manufacturing, wholesale, retail, and service businesses) and commercial bank customers. Generally, the models cover a specific geographic region, while some models, such as those for North America and Western Europe, have underlying industry-based modules.

The models use a variety of data elements that have been warehoused to accurately predict default probability directly or a rating that reflects a range of default probabilities. These include fundamental financial/credit analysis, company size and qualitative assessments. By taking the balance sheet and income statement of the company and boiling them down to a set of financial ratios that are common in credit analysis — such as the interest coverage ratio, the leverage ratio and the cash flow to debt ratio — we can use this information to help determine the credit worthiness or default likelihood of the customer. Ratios and inputs will vary from region to region and from industry to industry depending on factors such as accounting rules, local practices and, importantly, statistical significance.

Another key factor in determining default likelihood is the size of the company, which we have found to be correlated with credit quality: larger companies tend to have more financial flexibility (access to funding from many sources), more diverse revenue streams, customer base and geographic reach, and so forth. Depending on the specific model, the measure of size will be selected on a basis similar to the process for selecting the financial ratios. To the extent that we have history on more "qualitative" aspects of firms, such as market position, quality of management and infrastructure, and so forth, these data elements allow the modeler to "fine tune" the model for qualitative factors.

The first generation of models took the form of a model that tried to predict a given risk category and back out the probability of default utilizing simple linear regression. Currently, we still build and utilize models of this kind in which insufficient history does not allow direct modeling of default probability. But more and more, as we gather data and financial information on defaulted companies, we are able to model the probability of default directly. The key to building precise and statistically significant models is to gather both financial and qualitative data on defaulted companies — data such as the date of default, an understanding of why the default occurred and most importantly, the statement of accounts in the years preceding the default. This provides a more precise measure of risk assessment, as you are directly identifying the probability of default.

Originally, the models were delivered as a desktop application, and relied on an MS Access back end to warehouse all the data. Users were asked to input a limited balance sheet and income statement into the application, answer a selection of qualitative questions and then calculate the risk rating category. This method had severe limitations and was a catalyst for data collection and warehousing. For the credit analyst using the model to make a credit decision, the inability to easily and electronically share data was a limitation. For the modeler, the database that stored the data input was not centralized. This meant that whenever any new analysis or model validation was required, the modeler had to solicit the data from a variety of locations.

At Citigroup, we have model coverage for our portfolio across the globe, with as many as 3,000 users, so any kind of data collection effort became a tedious, time consuming process for a large amount of people. Identifying all users, soliciting their databases and having them sent to the modelers took considerable time, yet was a supported venture by all involved because the value of the data and the models that it would create was recognized.

The credit risk models are generally reestimated every three to five years, depending on performance and the volatility of the businesses covered. Every new release of the credit models includes increased sophistication with regard to the statistical analysis used to create the algorithm and with regard to the software. A key focus of new software development is how to simplify and improve the data warehousing. Finally, after much time and effort, a new credit risk model application was launched last year over a Citigroup-wide global network. One database will warehouse all the data that users from all over the globe enter into the model. This is the first step in building a real time data warehouse. The next step is implementing the models on an Internet-based platform, where the users would input information via a Web page, and all relevant data are warehoused and a risk category is provided. However, introducing a new global application is not a simple process and depends heavily on the information technology environment in all countries where Citigroup does business. So an application, either server or Web-based, that works seamlessly in New York, may be unusable in Kinshasa or Kuala Lumpur due to existing technological obstacles. Thus, the application must be designed with these variances in mind and tested extensively prior to implementation.

Not only does the data collected in real time allow modelers to build new models, it allows modelers to validate existing models — certainly a requirement of the new Basel II Accord (reviewed later in this chapter), which will allow qualifying banks to use internal ratings to set regulatory capital. With access to the data on an ongoing basis, we should be able to more quickly answer the question of whether or not the models are assigning the appropriate risk category to companies with declining credit worthiness. This aspect of validation is key to providing the risk managers, analysts and other users with tools that they can use to manage the risk of the portfolio and to identify problem customers. The most important validation of a credit model is via the collection of data on defaulted companies — this will let us see that the model is correctly assigning a more risky category to a weak credit. Ideally, you always want to observe a positive relationship between a more risky category and the incidence of default. This kind of validation allows us to adjust the model when appropriate, bearing in mind that the data used are yearly in frequency.

Early Warning Models

In addition to these fundamental models that measure credit risk, there are other kinds of models that can be built using the data that have been warehoused — models that provide early warning signals regarding default and deteriorating credit worthiness. They can fall into many categories, but we will discuss two:
1.   Models that measure default likelihood
2.   Models that measure changes in credit risk

These models are not used to assign risk categories to customers, but allow banks to monitor customers carefully and, generally, on a more frequent basis than fundamental credit risk models. Most importantly, they can provide an early signal that a credit is facing default or deterioration.

Default likelihood early warning models generate default likelihood estimates as output and can be built using company financial information, stock market information or a combination of the two. Because they mainly rely on stock market information as a data input, we can provide more up-to-date monitoring of the credit. Additionally, thousands of companies are listed on the U.S. exchanges, so a huge number of companies can be reviewed at one time.

Reliance on stock market data perhaps implies that the results will be less accurate than if the analysis was done on a company-by-company basis — as in the fundamental credit risk models discussed earlier. The stock market provides rich data that have significant information content regarding a company's health and welfare, but there is also much "irrational exuberance" embedded in the data, as well as other "noise" that may not speak directly to credit risk. Nonetheless, these models provide an efficient way to monitor both problem credits, as well as credits which may begin to deteriorate over time, for both the customer base and the non-customer base.

The second kind of early warning model focuses on change in credit quality. This "credit quality trend" model provides an estimate of the likelihood that the company's risk category or rating will be downgraded (i.e., the risk increases). This model is also built utilizing market information, so it has the same positive and negative issues with regard to using equity data to predict credit phenomena as the probability of default early warning models.

These models can be used for informational monitoring on a monthly basis and can be used to trigger reviews and investigation based on the results. As their use becomes more accepted and widespread, they can be used to trigger actual, policy-driven actions regarding the customer — such as limits on how much the bank can lend to the customer, required rating reviews and discussions with management of the customer.

The models are monitored on a monthly basis and accuracy and goodness-of-fit are objectively measured. Any changes that are deemed necessary because of the testing can be made as often as needed — this would generally be done on a monthly basis, since that is the frequency of the data being used in the testing. The default probability model is tested against new defaults that are identified to see if we have captured the defaults with a sufficiently high default likelihood. The credit quality trend model is also being objectively tested against publicly rated companies that have experienced significant degradation in their credit worthiness.

Measuring Loss

The second component of credit risk is the loss given default (LGD) for the portfolio of the bank. This does not represent a significant connection to data mining, but it is integral to risk assessment and goes hand-in-hand with the other true data mining activities described above. Generally, the loss given default refers to the loss the bank will incur from its exposure to a given customer in the event that the customer defaults. If a bank, for example, has an LGD of 40%, the bank, on average, can expect to lose 40 cents for every dollar of exposure to a defaulting customer. It is this piece of information, along with the credit risk category, that will enable the bank to calculate the amount of regulatory capital it will be required to hold — regulatory capital will be discussed in more detail later in the chapter.

There is a tremendous problem here with capturing the data necessary to perform this calculation. A large amount of detail is required on the specifics of the actual lending to calculate an accurate LGD, as well as a long history of defaults and the concurrent information about the lending.

Use of Information

In 2002, market watchers saw the credit worthiness of the corporate world at a low point. Countries defaulted, there were widespread defaults in various industries, like the telecom industry, and fraud-related defaults plagued the international markets. Even in this high default rate environment, the organizations suffering the most are not necessarily the banks, as one would expect. In this credit cycle, the banks have finally been able to use the information and analysis that they have been doing in a fruitful way. As banks have begun to understand the credit risk of their portfolios, they are creating new products, like credit derivatives, bundling the credit risk and selling it. As a result, the credit risk is no longer concentrated on the books of the banks, but rather, has been voluntarily spread amongst many insurance companies and pension funds, as they have purchased the derivative as an investment.

Future of Risk Assessment

One of the important aspects of data warehousing and model building is, as we have discussed, that the banks can make more informed decisions regarding the risk they hold on their balance sheets. They can identify the customers with which they want to do business, the level of risk they want to incur and make decisions regarding the management of the risk they are carrying. Other important factors that the banks will have to address are the fundamental reforms that are sweeping through the banking industry.

Currently, banks are required to keep a fixed amount of regulatory capital set aside for a credit event. This amount is regulated by the 1988 Basel Capital Accord of the Bank for International Settlements. The Basel Committee on Banking Supervision announced in June 1999 a proposal to replace the 1988 Capital Accord with a more risk-sensitive framework, the Basel II Accord. A second proposal was released in January 2001 that incorporated comments on the original proposal. The proposal is based on "three pillars" that would allow banks and regulators to evaluate various aspects of banking risk, including market, credit and operational risk. These include: minimum capital requirements, supervisory review and market discipline. The existing accord focuses on coming up with the total amount of bank capital, an amount that is important in preventing a bank from insolvency during a credit event. It uses an approach that does not benefit a bank that has any active risk management. For instance, a bank that actively seeks out very low risk customers will be required to hold the same amount of regulatory capital as a bank that does not manage its risk profile.

The new proposal seeks to expand this approach to include a variety of measures of risk, including a bank's own internal methodologies. For credit risk, there are two approaches: the Standardized approach and the Internal Ratings Based, or IRB, approach. The Standard approach is very similar to the existing Accord, but where the existing Accord only provides one risk weight, the Standard approach will provide four. The IRB approach is where banks who have been warehousing data and using it to build better credit risk models will benefit tremendously. This approach will allow banks to use their credit risk models in determining what amount of capital will need to be held. The approach is broken into two segments: foundation and advanced. In the foundation approach, a bank will be able to use the output of its credit risk models — the rating — which is associated with a likelihood of default, and the banking supervisor will provide the other inputs to calculate the capital requirement. In the advanced approach, a bank will use the output of its credit risk models and will be able to supply the other inputs as well. In addition to the probability of default, these inputs include loss given default, exposure at default and maturity.

Ideally, if a bank is managing its risk, it can reduce the amount of regulatory capital that it is required to hold. Because this approach provides significant benefit to banks that can prove the validity of their risk management system to their regulators, via detailed testing results and disclosure on the data and modeling used, there is much incentive to continue to warehouse data in the most efficient fashion and continue to build better, more precise credit risk models that utilize newer statistical techniques.

Consumer Lending

Consumer lending traditionally included house mortgages, car loans, personal loans, and so forth, managed at the local branch. The risk evaluation was very crude; there was little specificity in the risk assessment. Usually, the loans were treated alike and a common risk was assigned to them. However, with the help of the computer, the data collection started, which paved the way for tailored risk decisions. The decisions of extending a loan and then pricing it moved beyond the previous crude means and now were based on statistical models using the massive data sets compiled.

Nowadays, the newest methods, neural networks, may be utilized to evaluate the risk of customer lending. The models are constantly validated and updated by each loan activity — approved or rejected and defaulted or non-defaulted. These techniques can easily place the model building and updating activities into the hands of the banker, who only has to feed the key parameters of the next loan and those of the borrower into the neural network. The technique presents the accepted/rejected decision, which the banker is free to modify. The final decision about the approval is fed back into the system, where this extra information prompts the neural network to adjust and fine tune its decision-making process. The parameters of the defaulted loans are also fed into the system, which causes the decision-making process to adjust itself. Besides the widely used so-called "score-card," this flexible neural network approach has been gaining importance and it may provide a tailored decision-making process for each branch.

The revolution in consumer banking can also be seen in the widespread use of the automated teller machines (or ATMs). Behind those "money machines" there are high-powered data-bases, linking all accounts of a customer instantaneously with artificial intelligence.

The newest way of banking is online banking, which provides access to almost all services we used to obtain at a branch. Barring a few activities (e.g., withdrawing cash, getting a certified check), we can perform all banking transactions on our personnel computer. Online banking is not only a service to the customers, but it acts as a regular website, equipped with all marketing and artificial intelligence power.

Credit Card

Credit Card (which is a special, proliferated loan business) belongs to consumer banking, but it has become so large a business that we discuss it independently. The lucrative credit card business, in today's form, owes its existence solely to data warehousing and data mining. The business is only a few decades old (e.g., the predecessor of the Visa card was born in 1958), but it has grown into one of the most important segments of banking. A credit card is a revolving credit, where the customer pays an annual fee (which is waived at many institutions in today's competitive market) and interest on the borrowed amount, and the merchant pays a certain percentage on the purchase. The primary activity of the company that issues the credit card is information storage (recording each purchase of each credit card account), purchase authorization, billing and fee collection.

The amount of information gathered and stored is tremendous. Let us take a modest portfolio of 1 million credit card accounts and assume 30 purchases a month per each account. The portfolio will accumulate data on 360 million purchases within a short year, and each purchase will be described by many attributes (e.g., amount and time of purchase, type and location of store). Without any investment, adding all available internal data on the customers (e.g., activities of other bank accounts) can further enrich this precious data set. The data set is also enriched by adding information from external sources as well. Such data can be individual lifestyle and demographics information (e.g., buying preferences, various magazine subscriptions, residential information, etc.), or census data at the lowest possible level.

The ability to warehouse, link, and mine this information can lead to profitable and powerful business opportunities, and the possibilities are enormous. Accordingly, these colossal databases are useless unless we can extract the necessary knowledge from them. The various statistical techniques offered by data mining allow us to probe these huge files and create models for any kind of marketing activity. Let us review some of the main activities in the credit card operation. These activities are synchronized efforts between marketing and data analysis. The two sides affect each other by constant interaction and feedback. For example, marketing plans to solicit certain merchandise. Data mining can not only discover segments of the population receptive to that solicitation, but can describe various hidden attributes of those segments, which, in turn, can help marketing to position its product more effectively.

- **Acquisition:** Acquisition is the most fundamental activity that builds up the portfolios. Even though the local markets might be saturated, there is still opportunity by offering second or third cards, and the local portfolios can be expanded into global ones. Acquisition may target current customers or people from external sources. The successful acquisition campaigns target the potential customers with the help of statistical modeling, which predicts the highest possible rate of acceptance and conversion.

- **Retention:** Retaining existing customers is the cheapest way of acquisition and it gains importance as the market gets saturated. In a way, it complements acquisition. It analyzes the characteristics of those customers who cancelled their credit card accounts, and in the next wave of acquisitions, those types of customers can be identified in advance and special programs can be designed and directed at them to keep them active customers. For example, credit cards with special promotions (such as purchase reimbursement) can be offered.

- **Default management:** Managing risk in the credit card portfolio is as fundamental as in the corporate loan portfolio described in the first section of the chapter. Similar to the practices there, the collection and full analysis of the defaulting credit card accounts is the centerpiece of building statistical models to predict, minimize or avoid defaults. The knowledge learned from the defaulting accounts influence almost all activities in the portfolio.

- **Cross-selling:** A principal rule of marketing is, "Your own customers are your best customers." It is much more cost effective to sell a product to a current customer than to a non-customer. We collect huge amounts of high quality information on our own customers. The knowledge gained from mining this vast set of data provides many possible ways to offer our next product. But more importantly, our customers have already demonstrated loyalty, which increases our chances for success. Cross-selling involves the bank's various financial products (e.g., investment), but the bank can team up with other financial (e.g., insurance) and nonfinancial (e.g., travel) companies to solicit products of a different nature. Besides generating outright profit, cross-selling is also an opportunity to add more information to the customer database, making it more valuable for the next marketing campaign.

- **Boosting long-term value:** After maintaining a long relationship with the credit card customers, the bank possesses so much information that a statistical model can be developed to model the long-term value of the customer — as a credit card holder and as a general bank customer. The former may only rely on the credit card purchase history of the customer; the latter takes into consideration the activities in all accounts of the customer. The long-term value model should influence the cross-selling practices, since that value is the combination of all accounts and the optimum may be achieved, while the profit in one account is not the largest possible. The bank performs delicate research by linking all available data of a customer and sometimes learns information not directly translatable into profit, in order to boost customer loyalty. The virtue of restraining marketing efforts should also be exercised (e.g., let us not bombard the customer with solicitations of a low-profit product, when the customer may purchase a high-profit product).

- **Fraud detection:** Fraud detection protects both the bank itself and the customer. Credit card and identity theft is an increasing danger, which can be fought with the help of data mining. Utilizing various statistical methods, we can recognize unusual purchase patterns and act immediately. The purchase pattern recognition is based on some common rules applied to all customers utilizing *individual* purchase history data. The model is individually built, at least in the sense that a common framework takes the parameters or trigger values specific to a credit card account. Of course, the longer the credit card account has been active, the more reliable the fraud detection.

- **Selling customer data:** Data warehousing, data mining and capturing high quality information on long credit card usage gave birth to a new business within the credit card sector: information commerce or selling information on customers. First, we have to state that customers' privacy must be protected and selling information must be done within the legal and *ethical* constraints. Prudence has a selfish reason too: companies protect their best customers. Two types of activities can be differentiated based on the level of information sold: individual and summarized.

  • Selling mailing lists of defined properties (e.g., list of new parents, which could be compiled by identifying accounts of 20- and 30-somethings with sudden disappearance of restaurant use and concurrent appearance of pharmacy use, especially diaper purchases). Companies can easily find the segments of desired attributes in the databases.

• The databases can be researched for buyer's behavior, specific purchase patterns, merchandise preference, linking of merchandise, and so forth. This market research results in summarized information found in the database, not individual customer data as before. Other companies perform similar market research (let us think only of supermarket chains, which offer various discount cards not only to boost customer loyalty, but equally importantly, to gather precious data to facilitate market research).

• **Customer service, online account information:** Data warehousing makes flexible, multifaceted customer service possible. Besides providing a basic billing and account information service, it opens a new channel of marketing and selling various products. After the customer initiates the contact and obtains the necessary service, the system instantaneously directs the customer service representative to offer products in which the customer is likely to be interested.

Endnotes

• Bank for International Settlements, Basel Committee on Banking Supervision. (2001, January). *Overview of the new basel accord.*

• Ferguson, B. (2000). A consistent, global approach to risk. *The Journal of Lending and Credit Risk Management,* February, 20-24.

Editor's Notes

As you can see, the evolution of data, storage and analytic techniques has helped transform and augment a number of strategic functional activities within the banking sector. The effective utilization of quantitative and statistical methods incorporated in data mining can often lead to more efficient organizational operations. The past chapter clearly illustrated this concept by describing the benefits data mining and quantitative analytic techniques add to risk management activities in the world of lending. The next chapter will further address the topic of enhancing operational efficiency in lending practices and will focus more on activities in lending to small businesses. The concepts in the next section provide a more detailed illustration of managing risk in lending to small businesses through data mining and also extends to such topics as increasing market share (e.g., new customer acquisition) and overall profitability.

Chapter III

Credit Scoring and Risk Management for Small Business Lending

Vernon Gerety, PhD
PredictiveMetrics Inc., USA

Introduction to the Financial Services Industry

"The house always wins" is a common reprise for the empty pocket tourist leaving the gambling tables at Vegas. You do not need to be a professional gambler to understand that the house always wins because the odds are stacked in their favor. Unfortunately, the recent conditions in the financial services industry have been tighter than the quarter slot machines in the Vegas airport.

The financial services industry has been initiated with a never-ending ebb and flow between deregulation and "re-regulation". In general, the reaction to changing regulations has been an industry consolidation and the creation of global, national and super regional lending markets, replacing the traditional "brick and mortar" structure.[1] The restructuring of the financial markets has virtually eliminated the relevance of a "banking footprint", in which knowledge of the local economy and personal relationships was a key factor in managing risk. In today's environment, the lending officer's local market knowledge has dissipated and the relationship with the end user is more informal and often impersonal.

The inevitable intensifying competition has increased the cost of funds to the lender and lowered the interest rate paid by the borrower. The resulting lower margins have required that financial institutions lower costs by increasing efficiency and improving processes for customer acquisition and service. This transformation requires a change in both strategy and tactics, making the financial risk manager's job even more challenging.

Risk Management: The Art of Control

For the financial services industry, the balance between growth and profitability ultimately rests with an institution's risk management strategy. At the end of the day, losses make or break a lending institution's income statement. To better deal with this environment, the successful financial service companies are adopting advanced risk management strategies to manage and profitably grow their customer base.

A successful risk management strategy requires putting in place the necessary credit controls to maintain the portfolio's quality without stifling growth. The leading financial services companies have adapted knowledge-based decision systems as the foundation of their risk management strategy, in which these decision tools are used not only to make credit decisions faster, but over time the risk management profession has begun to appreciate that these advanced systems make better decisions.

Figure 1: Superior Risk Management Strategy

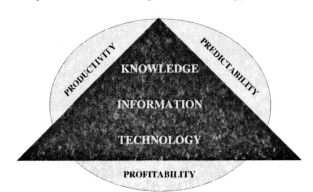

Figure 1 illustrates the key components of a successful knowledge-based system. The foundation of the knowledge-based decision system is technology. The information age has finally delivered on the promises of improved data management, leading to improved organizational processes such as customer acquisition, management and analysis. Technology in turn is the foundation that enables the financial institution to access a higher quantity of data. The next step in the pyramid is to understand the quality of data and to determine which data provide informational value in the decision process. Finally, the development of advanced decision algorithms such as logistic regression and segmentation classification techniques ensures the maximum value is extracted from the information available. The resulting knowledge-based system leads to improved tactical and strategic decisions.

The banking industry and larger financial services companies, such as GE Capital, have put into place corporate-wide risk management organizations to develop credit policy and monitor portfolio quality. These institutions have tremendous investment in knowledge-based decision systems to improve the control, consistency and ultimate credit decision-making process.

This chapter discusses the types of knowledge-based decision systems that are driven by statistically derived credit scoring algorithms specific to the small business lending market.

Small Business Lending:
Instant Decisions and the Winner's Curse

In general, within the small business lending marketplace the competitive pressure discussed above has created two related but opposing forces:

1. **Instant Approval:** The customer demands both fast decisions and instantaneous approvals. The small business applicant is typically looking for immediate delivery of the funds to satisfy an urgent need for working capital or to purchase a critical piece of equipment. Therefore, the institution with the fastest approval will increase its chances of "booking the deal".

2. **Winner's Curse:** Competition, however, also means a borrower will "shop the deal" with many lenders and the potential exists that the winner of the deal loses in the long term. The winner's curse is caused by competitive pressure that forces a lender to take greater risk than might be considered prudent to win the business. This is related to the concept of *adverse selection,* in which the unsuspecting lending institution is approving other lenders' rejects. So although you win the business today, the future increase in delinquency and losses is the penalty for making an uninformed credit decision. The winner's curse typically results from asymmetrical information

concerning the financial condition of the borrower and having inferior risk management strategies, low credit standards and/or poor credit processes.

The need for instant approvals while avoiding the winner's curse requires a credit process that is *both* automated and accurate. Therefore, sophisticated technology has been adapted to small business lending, specifically work flow technology and automated credit scoring models. The result is an application being processed in seconds rather than hours or days. The development of knowledge-based decision systems facilitates faster *and* better decisions and enables the lender to book more volume while avoiding being cursed with an underperforming portfolio.

Brief History of Credit Scoring

Credit scoring models, like all statistically designed forecasting tools, are based on the simple philosophy that "the past predicts the future". These statistical models are derived by analyzing current conditions and past behavior to predict future risk. Typically a credit-scoring model is designed to predict the likelihood of an applicant or customer being significantly delinquent in payments or being written off as a bad debt.

The use of credit scoring for underwriting has been utilized for several years for consumer lending, in which the high volume and low dollar transactions made it a perfect tool for assisting the credit card industry in a rapid growth of new customer acquisitions. [2]

For commercial underwriting the uniqueness of financial transactions has led to a much slower growth in the use of credit scoring.

The productivity gains were not as evident when the number of transactions was smaller and the value of the deal was higher relative to consumer lending.

However, despite the early resistance by commercial lenders to credit scoring, the growth in the small business lending market has created a perfect environment for leveraging its application. The small business loan is a hybrid of both consumer and commercial lending. Most small businesses are sole proprietors that generate all their personal income from their business and the transactional value of the lending relationship is very similar to consumer credit. However, the ability of small businesses to pay back the loan is dependent on the success of the business.

By the early 1990s, several leading financial commercial lenders were utilizing credit scoring to automate the credit process for managing the rapid growth in the small business lending market.

Small Business Lending: Adapting to Credit Scoring

Similar to consumer lending, credit scoring for small business lenders was initially used to improve the speed and efficiency of the credit process, especially for the smaller dollar transactions. Traditional credit professionals believed that a trained credit analyst would, *ceritus paribus*, make a better decision than a statistically derived algorithm. However, with advances in estimation techniques, improved data sources and improved technology, this attitude has changed to the point at which scoring is no longer viewed as an inferior substitute for a credit analyst, but an automated tool that provides a more consistent, accurate decision that increases the effectiveness of the credit analyst and improves long-term portfolio quality.

The greater accuracy of credit scoring comes from the power of sophisticated analytical techniques to evaluate hundreds of credit risk data elements to find the most predictive set of data elements and then optimally weighting them to maximize the score's predictiveness. These more sophisticated scoring techniques, when combined with ever-improving access to information, have greatly improved the predictive ability and speed of the decision.

Utilization of credit scores provides the foundation for developing a consistent decision process that allows trained credit analysts to focus their time on the more difficult credits not easily decided by credit scoring, which include firms with limited history or unique financing needs. The inherent consistency and control that is offered by leveraging a statistical score in the credit process has fueled the rapid growth in the small business lending market.

Applications of Credit Scoring

Credit scoring in the small business lending market has been utilized for a variety of applications including marketing, customer acquisition, portfolio management and maximizing existing customer relationship.

Figure 2 provides a description of the applications of credit scoring for small business lending. Specific applications of credit scores include pre-screening prospects to determine creditworthiness, automating new account decisions, monitoring an active customer base and setting credit lines to increase the share of wallet for existing customers with superior credit.

Figure 2: Applications of Scoring Solutions Across the Customer Lifecycle (Source: V. Gerety & M. Metroka (2002, Oct.). "The Future of Leasing.")

Targeting

☐ Overlay scores on portfolio for targeted pre-qualified & cross-sell efforts
☐ Provide pre-qualified names to sales

Maximizing

☐ Help loan expiration
☐ Identify cross-sell and up-sell opportunities
☐ Adjust credit lines

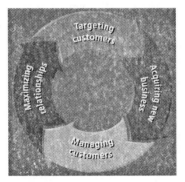

Acquiring

☐ Process new applications
☐ Bulk portfolio purchases

Managing

☐ Monitor portfolio
☐ Track customer credit risk
☐ Determine overall portfolio risk
☐ Prioritize collections

New Application Processing: Processing new credit applications is the most common application of credit scoring. In these circumstances, the lending institution has no past history with the applicant and must rely on external data, typically credit bureau and/or financial data, to make a credit decision.[3]

More advanced uses of scoring to acquire new customers include using credit scores to: (1) assist in the credit due diligence for portfolio purchases and (2) pre-screening prospects to support sales and marketing efforts.[4]

Portfolio Management: An increasingly popular application of credit scoring is managing a portfolio of customers. The scores are generated on all customers based upon internal and external data. The scores are refreshed periodically, typically monthly or quarterly, for all customers with whom the institution currently has an active lending relationship. The scores are used to determine the credit quality of the entire active customer base. These types of scores are used to make decisions on new loans with existing customers, monitor the credit quality of the portfolio, determine collection strategy, and to better forecast delinquency and loss.

Types of Models and Scores

The application of credit scoring discussed above is specific to the type of model developed. This section discusses specific types of credit scoring models and scores commonly used by small business lenders.

Credit Scoring Models

Credit scoring models provide the capability to immediately assess the risk that a prospect, new applicant or existing customer will become severely delinquent, be written-off, experience bankruptcy, or exhibit some other type of derogatory payment behavior over a specified period of time. The model is often customized using the lender's actual portfolio of customers and therefore is consistent with the lender's business goals and objectives.

An effective credit scoring system incorporates the relevant data available specific to a firm's current financial health. The most sophisticated systems combine internal lender data, external bureau data (commercial and consumer), and the lender's financial statement data (especially for larger exposures). Within the small business lending sector, additional sources of industry specific loan payment data have been developed that will provide significant "lift" in predictive ability of these rating systems.

Broad types of credit scoring models include:

- **New Application Scoring Model:** A new application scoring model is designed to score applicants with no prior history with a lender. New application models are the most common type of credit scoring model utilized for small business lending.
- **Behavior Scoring Model:** A behavior model provides the capability to quickly and accurately evaluate the risk of future payment behavior of an existing customer. Behavior models are typically the most powerful statistical tools and allow for the highest percentage of accuracy and precision in prediction power.

Types of Credit Scores

There are several types of scores that are available for various credit purposes. This section discusses three broad types of credit scores commonly being utilized in the financial services market.

- **Generic Risk Scores:** These scores are developed on a broad cross-section of business behavior. The scores are typically based upon trade payment behavior, predicting 90-plus day delinquency within a 12-month performance window. These scores are predominately offered by the credit bureaus.[5] They usually are developed on a large, random sample of all businesses in the bureau's database and are marketed to be representative of the business market.

   Generic scores are effective general risk assessment tools and are especially valuable for companies that market to a broad cross-section of industries. For example, many telecommunication and utilities companies have found generic scores to be effective for new customer underwriting. They are also useful for companies that need a risk management score ideally fitted to a commercial niche, but lack the resources to develop and maintain a score fitted to their specific business. In this case the score's effectiveness may not be as great as a custom solution, but still provides much needed intelligence.

Generic scores, although easy to implement and typically lower cost, can be too general for the needs of most small business lenders. If they are utilized, they are typically only an ingredient in a much broader set of rules and criteria to "customize" to the unique requirements of the small business lender. This usually results in a higher percentage of applications needing to be reviewed by credit analysts. Lenders are therefore highly desirous of solutions that are fitted to their industry, and even more so, customized to their own business.

- **Industry Scores:** As suggested by their name, these scores are designed for a particular industry, such as small business lending. The scores are very explicit to the industry's actual credit practice and performance experience. They are developed by sampling creditor behavior from a specific industry and are developed to predict how customers of that industry will pay for the products and services sold in that industry.[6] For example, a pooled small business lending score will predict how lenders will be paid on small business loans. Clearly, these scores are designed for the lender's specific risk assessment needs. In most cases, they provide a higher level of predictive power than generic scores.

  These scores are very powerful because they are based upon the mix of customers, the type of credit and the payment habits of customers within a specific industry. They are especially valuable when the industry's type of customers and credit product is significantly different relative to the business universe.

Industry scores are beneficial if the lender does not have a sufficient quantity of new or existing accounts to build a custom model or if they are changing their marketing strategy and the existing portfolio is not representative of the future business they will be evaluating and acquiring.

These scores, although they tend to be less predictive than a custom solution discussed below, may be more stable, especially if the economic climate, the lender's market strategy and/or the types of credits being evaluated changes.

- **Custom Scores:** The most precise type of score is derived from a custom model solution. These scores are based upon models developed using *only* the individual company's sample of customers. They tend to be the most predictive since they are based upon the actual experience of a specific company's portfolio. These scores are designed to mirror the "through the door" sample of applications, to predict how the company is being paid by actual customers.

  Custom scores can provide the lender with a strong competitive advantage. These scores are based upon the lender's own performance and are proprietary to their operations. Therefore, the improved predictive power of custom scores provides the lender a competitive edge by enabling them to identify and approve better credits. An effective score can lead to higher approval rates with lower delinquency and losses.[7]

  The major drawback of custom scores is the significant amount of time and expense, both external and internal, required to develop and implement custom models. In addition, periodic maintenance, (typically every one to two years) is required to ensure the scores maintain the level of predictive accuracy needed to secure peak performance.[8]

Figure 3: Pros & Cons of Various Score Types (Source: V. Gerety & M. Metroka (2002, Oct.). "The Future of Leasing." The Monitor.)

Score Type	Pros	Cons
Generic Scores	• Ease to obtain and implement • Minimal startup cost • Good general risk tool for many business & industries • Excellent for net 30 trade credit • Good 'starter' score for firms inexperienced with scoring	• Potentially less predictive of non-trade financing • Less "no touch" potential leading to a manual credit process • Less effective for long term credit
Industry Scores	• Based upon the typical mix of business found in specific industry • Predicts the industries customer's payment behavior • Good for benchmarking payment patterns internally versus the competition • May be more robust than custom models if economic, market conditions or strategies are changing frequently • Especially appropriate for firms big enough to benefit from scoring but not big enough to develop a custom solution	• Will be less applicable to 'niche' firms or markets • Tend to be less predictive than custom • Eliminates competitive advantages for the industry leaders who can leverage custom solutions
Custom Scores	• Most often the best scoring solution for large high volume industry leaders • Specific to firms individual business experience • Designed, developed and implemented to be consistent with overall business strategy and goals	• Resource intensive. Requiring a significant amount of both internal & external investment • Significant upfront development and maintenance cost • May be less robust and more unstable if economic, market or business strategies change rapidly

Also, the strength of the industry score is a weakness of a custom score. If the economic climate changes, the lender's market strategy changes and/or the types of credits being evaluated changes, the lender may lose the advantage gained by using a custom solution. That is why score validation and maintenance are so important when employing a custom solution. See Figure 3 for a summary of the pros and cons of the various types of credit scores discussed in this section.

In summary, scoring models come in many types and levels of effectiveness depending on your need. The business needs to understand its specific risk and credit environment and evaluate which scoring solution works best for its particular need.

Developing Credit Scoring Models: Database Design and Model Development

All predictive models rely upon the past experiences to predict the future. Therefore, data on the recent past, which will be relevant for predicting the near future, is a necessary ingredient in the development of credit scoring models. The development of commercial credit scoring systems requires a sophisticated system of information and analytics to better understand the risk level of each deal. Three areas that are necessary and sufficient for a successful credit scoring system are:

1. **Information Utilization:** Use the information available more intelligently, extracting the maximum predictive value from the data acquired. Historically, financial services companies have attempted to minimize the investment in external data to

control cost. This strategy is proving to be the classic "penny wise but pound foolish" one, as industry leaders make improvements in decision capability by investing in improved information resources.

2. **New Information Sources:** Leverage new information sources to better understand loan risk and its potential profitability. Continuous improvement in technology and the proliferation of data on the Internet provide the decision maker with new and improved information sources.

3. **Superior Analytics:** The better utilization of data and understanding the value of new information sources requires comprehensive analytics to measure actual performance relative to the information available. The analytics will be used to develop scoring models that are performance based and can be effectively linked to the probability of severe credit loss.

The combination of more and better information is the foundation of adopting a superior risk management strategy that can significantly improve the predictive power of credit scoring models.

When developing a database for estimating a credit scoring model, the recent past must be considered to determine the impact on the models to be developed. The possibility that the user of the scoring model has recently entered a new market, introduced new products, has changed or will change marketing strategy along with the ups and downs of the economic cycles, can reduce or even invalidate the effectiveness of the credit scoring model.[9] Therefore, the data used to develop the model and the database structure are critical to the successful development of all predictive statistical models.

For credit scoring models, there exist three unique "windows" that define the structure of the data required. The data set is divided into three unique categories, denoted as "windows" in credit scoring terminology.

The *Observation Window* represents the point at which the customer is observed for predicting his or her future behavior. The *Performance Window* is the period that determines the performance the model is designed to predict. The *Historical Window* is derived by gathering information on the business from the recent past, specific to the financial institution's own relationship with that business, such as other loans approved that are currently active or recently paid off.

The *Observation Window* is the point at which the customer or applicant is observed for derivation of the credit score. The observation window is the point in time that the actual statistical prediction is generated. In other words, we are observing a specific point in the past and determining, based upon all the information available at that point in time, what the key factors are to predict future payment performance of that business. For that reason, the design of the database for the development of the model begins with the extraction of the records from the period of time chosen to be the observation window.

Ideally you would gather 12 unique months of observation to develop a credit scoring model. This would provide a more robust and stable statistical model that is less impacted by seasonal and cyclical changes that might occur over the 12-month period.

The *Performance Window* is the "future" behavior that the model is trying to predict. The performance window is used to determine which accounts are *good* versus *bad* credit risks. The performance window consists of the 12 to 24 months after the observation window. Within the performance window, data are gathered to determine whether the firm that was evaluated in the observation window was a bad or good risk based upon payment performance. The length of the performance window is dependent on the type of credit the model is based upon.

The *Historical Window* represents the most recent past for the customer. It is the period of time prior to the observation window. It is typically 6 to 12 months, and is used to understand the recent trends and habits in customer behavior. The historical window is only relevant for active customers where past behavior is observable. Therefore, historical windows are only constructed when the model is being developed on active customers. This is a specific type of model commonly referred to as behavior models, which will be discussed in more detail below.

As illustrated in Figure 4, the three "windows" discussed above work in tandem to build credit scoring models. Credit scoring models are designed to predict the behavior of customers

Figure 4: Credit Scoring Model Development Data Set Design

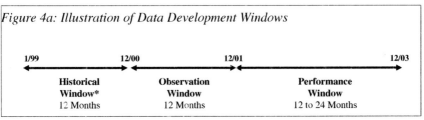

Figure 4a: Illustration of Data Development Windows

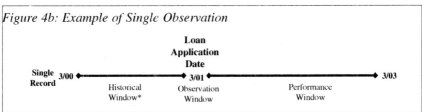

Figure 4b: Example of Single Observation

* Historical Window is only relevant if the firm is an existing customer with prior payment history at the point of observation.

observed in the observation window. The current state of the customer is observed in the observation window. It is important to note that customers included in the development sample from the observation window will be only good accounts. All available internal and external information available on the business is gathered for that specific point in time. For active customers with past payment history, additional data are added from observations in the historical window. The goal of the model is to identify accounts that will remain good versus accounts that will go bad over the performance window.

An example of a single observation is illustrated in Figure 4b. There a company applied for credit in March 2001. For this particular observation the record would be included in the development database because the application for credit was received during the observation window. If the loan was approved and booked, data concerning customer payments on the loan would be extracted forward 24 months from April 2001 through March 2003 to construct the performance window for that observation.

If the firm was already an existing customer with active loans on the books, than data on past payment habits would be gathered to understand "historical" performance for that observation to create the historical window. For this specific observation, detailed monthly data from March 2000 through February 2001 would be extracted. In addition, for a more comprehensive picture of the firm, summary data across the entire life of the relationship would be gathered. Examples of this include tenure of the firm as a customer, worst ever delinquency, and type of products purchased by customer.

Finally, if external bureau data were going to be appended, the data would need to be a snapshot of that customer for the time period March 2001, to correspond to the time period in which the original credit evaluation occurred and hence the point of observation for sampling for the modeling data.

Bad Definition: Defining a bad account is an important step in the model development process. The bad definition is usually based upon an account becoming severely delinquent over a 12 to 24 month performance window. "One-time 90-plus days past due including write-off and bankruptcy over the next 12 months" is a common form for a bad definition. Accounts that do *not* reach that state of delinquency, or they never have a delinquent payment beyond 89 days or experience a write-off during the 12 months in the performance window, are denoted as good accounts.[10]

The bad definition needs to be an event severe enough to be meaningful; having an adverse effect on the portfolio's quality, but not so severe that the number of bad ratings available for modeling is too limited to develop statistically significant and robust models. Since the credit scoring models are designed to predict the future likelihood of the bad event, it is critical that the bad definition is an event to be avoided. The goal is to have an early warning system that provides sufficient warning to avoid or reduce the chance the account will actually go bad.

Model Segmentation: An important step in the development of credit scoring models is to define the key segments within the portfolio of customers. Segmentation naturally occurs when the models are designed for separate purposes, such as evaluating new customers versus existing customers (see discussion below). But, within a dataset of common sets of businesses, other advanced statistical methods are used to determine the appropriate segmentation of accounts.

For commercial modeling, accounts might be segmented by the size of the firm (e.g., number of employees less than 10 vs. number of employees greater or equal to 10), customer type (e.g., retail vs. middle market), product type (e.g., secured vs. unsecured lending), and age of firm (e.g., firms less than three years vs. firms more than three years).

The goal is to determine the segments in which the individual customers are homogenous in terms of characteristics and behavior. In technical terms, segmentation identifies statistical relationships that are unique to the specific homogeneous segment. Proper segmentation will greatly improve the overall predictive power of the scoring model and ultimately the decision system for customers.

After model development, the data set and segmentation, the next step is to develop the specific models. The credit scoring model is derived from a statistical analysis of individual account credit performance. The purpose of the statistical analysis is to find the most predictive set of data elements that separate the good credit risks from the bad credit risks. Then the data elements are weighted statistically, using a multivariate statistical technique and an assumed distribution of risk, such as the logistic distribution, which is particularly well suited for the good versus bad credit risk class of problems.[11]

The greater accuracy of scoring models comes from the power of mathematics being able to analyze hundreds of credit risk data elements to find the most predictive set of data elements and then optimally weighting those elements to maximize the model's predictive power.

Developing Credit Scoring Models: Specific Model Types

New Application Scoring Model: As discussed, a new application scoring model is designed to score applicants with no prior history with a lender. These types of models are constructed by creating an observation window of new applications. Ideally, a minimum of 12 months of new applications are included in the development of a new application model. Payment information that occurs after the observation window specific to the lender by the borrower is gathered in the performance window. This information is used to determine which accounts are good versus bad risks. For small business lending, especially secured long-term lending, the performance window is typically 24 months.

Various types of information can be utilized when estimating a new application scoring model, including application data, financial data, and credit bureau data, including commercial and consumer credit bureau if appropriate. Statistical analysis is used to determine what set of data elements are the most predictive in evaluating credit risk.

The following types of data are commonly analyzed and scored by a new application scoring model: size of financing, payment terms, product type, and credit bureau data including firm charac-

Figure 5a: Predictive Data Elements — External Bureau & Financial Information

Commercial	Consumer	Financial
◆ Company History	◆ Average Trade Balance	◆ Leverage
◆ Credit Rating	◆ Charge-Offs	◆ Working Capital
◆ Industry/Geography	◆ Collection Inquiries	◆ Net Liquid Balance
◆ Negative Payment Experiences	◆ Credit Limit	◆ Net Worth
◆ Payment Index	◆ Current Balance	◆ Solvency Ratios
◆ Previous Bankruptcy	◆ Delinquent Trade Lines	◆ Cash Position
◆ Secured Financing	◆ Inquiries	◆ Profit Returns
◆ Size of Company	◆ Public Records	◆ Industry Norm Information
◆ Suits/Liens/Judgmnts	◆ Time on File	
◆ UCC Filings	◆ Total Trades	
◆ Years in Business		

teristics such as age and size of the firm, public court records such as recent suits, liens and judgments, and past payment patterns, with more weight given to recent payment history with other lenders. See Figure 5a for a more comprehensive list of data elements that are often included in various types of scoring models, including new application models.

New Application Models and Reject Inference: A unique component of new application models is the inability to observe the payment performance of accounts that are declined or rejected for credit. Unfortunately, rejects can make from 30% to 70% of new application's population, depending on the type of credit and borrower. Clearly the pool of rejects compared to the pool of approvals cannot be considered homogeneous. Typically, the rejects are much poorer credits and their characteristics and behavior are more consistent with the future bad event the model is designed to predict.

Therefore in order to build statistically representative and effective models, the issue of credit rejects must be dealt with. The treatment of rejects in credit scoring modeling is commonly referred to as *reject inference*. There are many advanced statistical methods to deal with rejects. But for the purpose of this discussion it is sufficient to mention that when new application models are developed, rejects must be included in the sample in order to get a true representation of the mix of applications that will be scored by the model. Typically rejects are added into the development sample as bad ratings and are included to obtain a more realistic estimation of the actual bad rate that would be observed on the "through the door" population of future scored new applications.[12]

Behavior Scoring Model: As discussed, a behavior model provides the capability to quickly and accurately evaluate the risk of future payment behavior of an active customer. Behavior models rely primarily on the financial services company's internal data and payment experience by the existing customer.

Behavior scoring models are typically based on 36-48 months of detailed customer attribute and accounts receivable data. The data are organized as a panel data set, incorporating both a cross-sectional and time series aspects of the customer portfolio.

When developing behavior scoring models, the reliance on internal customer data, especially past payment behavior with the lending institution, is extremely important. The information that is typically analyzed and incorporated into a behavior scoring model includes: historical internal performance data including current and historical A/R, tenure as a customer, type of loan(s), term and total exposure with the lender. See Figure 5b for a more comprehensive list of internal customer data elements that are often included in behavior scoring models.

The observation window is typically 12 months and represents the point at which the customer is observed. To help understand the trend in customer behavior the same customer is observed for up to 12 consecutive months. This repetitive observation sequence is what causes the observation window to be 12 months. The

Figure 5b: Predictive Data Elements: Behavior Models — Internal Accounts Receivable (A/R) & Customer Information

▢	Account Tenure	▢	Pay-Off Rate
▢	Collection Effort	▢	Payment Terms
▢	Credit Balance	▢	Payment Trend
▢	Current Aging		
▢	Date of Last Payment	▢	Sales Amounts
▢	Historical Aging	▢	Service Charges
▢	Late Fees	▢	Unpaid Late Fees
▢	NSF Checks	▢	Write-Off Amounts
▢	Past Due Days		

customer's 12 separate records are treated as independent observations. The historical window is unique to behavior models and is a time series representation back in time from the observation window. The historical window is typically 6 to 12 months and provides an important historical perspective of the customer's past financial services and payment behavior. Payment information that occurs after the observation window, specific to the lender by the borrower, is gathered in the performance window. This information is used to determine which accounts are good versus bad risks.

Figure 6 illustrates an example of one observation month for a behavior model database design. Customers A, B and C all have a history prior to the observation month. (G) denotes a customer in good standing while (B) denotes a customer in bad in the specific month. Based upon that month of observation, Customer (C) would be excluded from the sample for that month because it was bad within the observation window.

Note that there are two separate observations for Customer (A), which represent two separate loans that were booked at two

Figure 6: Credit Model Development — Database Design

	12/00					11/01			12/01	1/02							12/03
	Historical Window 12 Months								Observation Window 1 Month	Performance Window 24 Months							
Time Period	-12	-11	-10	-9	*	-3	-2	-1	0	1	2	3	*	21	22	23	24
Cust A – L1	G	G	G	G	*	G	G	G	G	G	G	G	*	G	G	G	G
Cust B	G	G	G	G		G	G	G	G	G	G	G	*	G	B	B	B
Cust C			G	G	*	G	B	B	B	G	G	G	*	G	G	G	G
Cust A – L2												G	*	G	G	B	B

G: Account currently in Good standing
B: Account currently in BAD standing

different points in time. For Customer (A), the first observation (L1) has been on the books over 36 months, while the second loan (L2) has been on the books only 22 months. The combination of both loans (L1 and L2) should be used to evaluate the total relationship for Customer A. For the first loan, Customer (A's) payment performance has been good during the performance window. However, for the second loan, Customer (A's) payment performance was bad. The total relationship for Customer (A) would most likely be considered bad if you combined the performance of Loan 1 and Loan 2.

External data take on significantly less importance in these types of models compared to new application models. In fact, several examples exist in which very predictive behavior models have been developed exclusively using internal data specific to the financial services company's own portfolio. Therefore, behavior scoring models have the added benefit of reducing the cost of purchasing external data for application processing and risk management review; however, external behavior will add some predictive value in terms of external validation of payment behavior and other risk factors.

Information Available on the Small Business

When developing a credit scoring model, the type of data available on the small business entity will be a major factor in determining the information used to develop a credit scoring model. The most predictive models will have the maximum amount of predictive information available to make a risk assessment. Unfortunately, market and regulatory factors limit the amount of data available on a small business. As was discussed above, the close link between the small business owner's personal and business financing makes it a unique area for utilizing both consumer and commercial data in the development of credit scoring models.

Many financial services companies rely exclusively on commercial data for small business credit underwriting. However, this approach may be missing the mark by not incorporating consumer data to increase decision accuracy and automation. Deals are lost and inferior decisions are being made because credit analysts are spending unnecessary time analyzing the creditworthiness of a company by relying on commercial data that is not extensive or is very limited.

In terms of predictive variables, three types of models have been developed for small business risk assessment depending on the data available:

- **Commercial Model:** A commercial model is one that is based upon external commercial bureau data on the business applicant.[13] The typical business that is scored using this model usually has significant business tenure and several trade payments on the external commercial credit bureau database. In many cases, the information available is inadequate to make an effective credit decision. Therefore, other data sources must be utilized to develop effective credit scoring models.

- **Blended Model:** Blended Models are algorithms that blend two unique data sources together. In small business lending for new applications credit evaluation, a common blend is commercial and consumer bureau data. These blended models are very powerful decision tools for small business financing. There are many small and start-up businesses that are either not in the commercial databases or have very little commercial information available with limited predictive power. In order to raise start-up and generate working capital, these small business owners often must rely on leveraging personal credit to meet the capital needs of their business. Therefore, a model that "blends" both commercial and consumer data to predict commercial behavior is a very effective risk management tool. In fact, within the small business marketplace, consumer data are often more predictive than limited commercial data. These types of models are especially important for partnerships, sole proprietorships and closely held private corporations.

- **Consumer Model:** A consumer model designed to predict commercial payment behavior is an effective tool when the business is very small, has just opened for business or cannot be found on the commercial bureau databases.

  The model is based upon the assumption that the way individuals manage personal finances will be indicative of the way they manage their business. Therefore, good personal credit translates into good business credit. The models are also typically used when the business owner is personally guaranteeing the financial transaction for the business. Depending on the type of credit (e.g., loan, lease or credit card), this may represent 30% to 90% of applications received, which should only increase with the emergence of the Internet as an online 24-hour sales channel.

  Strictly using consumer bureau data to make commercial lending decisions is a tricky and slippery slope for risk managers. Regulatory issues, sales concerns and risk management apprehensions are significantly inhibiting the use of these models.[14] Rarely is a commercial lending decision made exclusively on the basis of purely consumer bureau data alone. At a minimum, to avoid fraud, the existence of the business is validated using other third-party sources, such as bank or trade references, state business records, or even a copy of a utility bill, which includes the name and address of the business. Unfortunately, these other data sources are usually "offline" and require a manual intervention. Therefore, the ability to automate the decisions is lost.

Credit Scoring and Economic Cycles

An often suspected "limitation" of predictive tools, especially those based upon credit scoring, is the inability of these systems to deal with the ups and downs of the economic business cycle. The naysayers of credit scoring cite the pearls and certain doom of relying on a credit score during economic downturns. It is true that predicting the "turning point" of an economic business cycle is difficult even for the most sophisticated econometric models. However, a credit scoring system based upon the individual performance of businesses is probably the most effective way of dealing with the ups and downs of an economic cycle. While the salient points of this observation are too robust to fully develop in this chapter, it is sufficient to note the following about economic business cycles and credit scoring systems.

1.   Business cycles of expansion and contraction are based upon the behavior of economic units including individual consumers and businesses. The micro events of the economic units drive the macro statistics that make up the economic business cycle. Therefore, since credit scoring is based upon the micro behavior of individual firms, the models are more adept to picking up slight changes in economic behavior.

2.   A credit scoring system will react to an economic slowdown with an observed increase in the percentage of firms that are

scored poorly, resulting in an automated decrease in approval rates. The reduction in approval rates is exactly the correct strategy that should be employed during an economic downturn to avoid increases in delinquency and losses resulting from a weakening economy.

3.   The credit scores will still be able to "rank order risk", with the firms in the high-risk classes still generating the highest delinquency and losses. However, the bad rates will go up across all credit scores. This will require that credit policy be adjusted to maintain portfolio quality; typically the "cutoff" score for an approval is raised to lower overall approval rates.

In conclusion, credit scoring systems do not fall apart during an economic downturn. In fact, the change in the distribution of risk should be used by lenders as an early warning indicator of a potential economic slowdown that will have a negative impact on portfolio quality. However, it is important to closely monitor and adjust to changes in the economic business cycle. In fact, it could as easily be argued that developing automated scoring systems will allow lenders to adjust and react more quickly and accurately to changing economic conditions.

Case Studies: Credit Scoring for Small Business Lending

This section will present case studies of how credit scoring is being used to improve risk management within the small business lending market.

Utilizing Various Data Sources for Credit Scoring

The following case study illustrates the value of using multiple data sources to predict small business payment performance. This case study is based on a financial institution that specializes in small business lending.

The financial services company developed three separate credit scoring models to ensure 100% coverage for all decisions. The three models included a Commercial Only model based upon commercial bureau data only, a Consumer Only model based upon consumer bureau data from the business owner(s) and the third model is a "Blended" Model that combines commercial and consumer bureau data.

The performance and effectiveness of the models can be evaluated and compared by analyzing each model's credit screening and separation effectiveness. To measure credit-screening effectiveness we use the credit scoring model to calculate the probability of bad credit performance. As discussed above, typically "bad" is defined as severe delinquency or loss looking forward 24 months from the date of application.

The sample of accounts is sorted by score, where the score is derived from the probability of the account going bad over the performance window.[15] The result is a ranking of accounts from greatest risk to least risk. After sorting the accounts by score, the top 10% of the sorted accounts are in the top 10th percentile of greatest risk, the top 20% of the sorted account are in the top 20th percentile of greatest risk, and so forth. The credit screening effectiveness is identified by the proportion of known bad ratings captured at any percentage point within the ranked distribution of risk.

Figure 7 shows the credit screening effectiveness of each model. It provides percentiles along the x-axis and the percent of known bad ratings captured along the y-axis (bad %). In other words, the x-axis predicts who will be rated as bad and the y-axis tells you who actually went bad. The graph is demonstrating how effective the models are in predicting the future bad ratings.

To illustrate how to read Figure 7, consider the points on the commercial model curve. At the 30th percentile the commercial model captured 53% of the future bad ratings. The commercial model is able to screen out 53% of the bad ratings within the 30% of firms that the model predicted would be the highest risk. Obviously the higher percentage of bad ratings screened out, the greater the effectiveness of the model.

Figure 7 also illustrates the power of consumer bureau data in predicting small business behavior. In fact, for this specific ex-

Figure 7: Small Business Credit Scoring Models — New Account Model Case Study — Bad Capture Performance

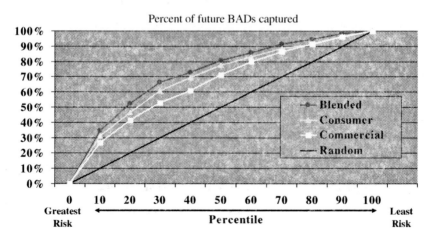

ample, the model developed using consumer bureau data only is actually more predictive than the commercial only model. At the 30th percentile, while the commercial model captured 53% of the future bad ratings, the consumer model captures 61% of the future bad ratings. Finally, the blended model demonstrates how more information is always better than less; the blended model captures 66% of the future bad ratings within the highest 30% of highest risk firms.

The financial impact is easily demonstrated by a simple illustrative example. Assume that the models are asked to evaluate 1,000 new financial services transactions in which 10% of 100 deals end up going bad.

If the financial services company approved 70% of all deals relying exclusively on the credit score, the financial services company would be able to avoid 53 bad ratings using the commercial model, 61 of the bad ratings using the consumer model and 66 bad ratings using the blended model. If all the bad ratings go to loss and the average loss is $8,000, then the commercial model will reduce losses by $488,000 (= 61 X $8,000), the consumer model will reduce losses by $424,000 (= 53 X $8,000), while the blended model will result in $528,000 (= 66 X $8,000) of loss avoidance. Clearly the model that screens out the highest percentage of bad ratings ensures the best portfolio quality.

This case study demonstrates that a multiple model solution is the most effective way to ensure the highest percentage of automation with the minimum impact on portfolio performance. The conclusion is that a blended model, with both consumer and commercial data, is the most effective credit tool for small, privately held companies.

Developing Risk Grades to Better Understand Profitability

Adopting a knowledge-based risk management strategy is designed to maximize profits, not simply manage risk. However, the management of risk is the key component of a financial services company's profitability.

A risk management strategy is based on an information approach, which is designed to better understand the risk of each deal and how each deal "fits into" the portfolio of deals that are being evaluated, approved and booked. Figure 8a provides an illustrative example of how using credit scoring in combination with other policy rules can be used to more effectively understand the risk levels of new applications and existing customers. The combination of credit scores and policy rules are used to create a risk grade for each customer; the grades assigned include A, B, C, D, F, with A being low risk and F being extremely risky customers.

Figure 8a also illustrates how the risk grades can be used to automate the credit decision process for new applications. In this example, A, B, and C credits are lower risk accounts that are automatically approved, F credits are extremely high risk accounts that are automatically declined, and D credits are marginal credits that require a manual review by a credit analyst. Typically, D credits are approved only if other information, not available to the scoring model, is available that supports approval or the deal is restructured to mitigate the risk of a D credit. Otherwise D credits are declined.

The graphs in Figure 8b show the distribution and performance of approved and booked loans by a custom designed risk grade. In Figure 8b, an additional risk grade "E" was added; for this case

Figure 8a: Using Risk Grades To Automate Credit Decisions

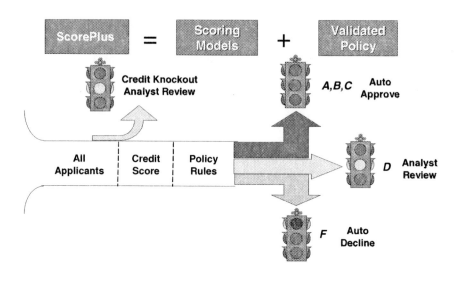

Figure 8b: Distributions Of Booked Applications and Loss Rate By Risk Grade

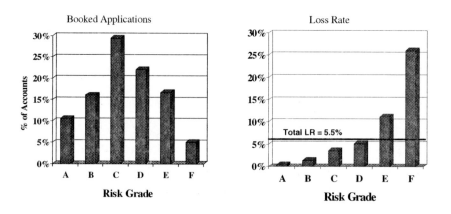

study, accounts that are graded D are subject to analyst review with a system recommendation of conditional approval depending on the ability to structure or price the deal more favorably. Risks that are grade E are subject to analyst review with a system recommendation of decline; accounts that are approved would be situations in which the data that were used to derive the score are refuted or additional information not available to the scoring model was provided, such as financial statement data showing substantial positive net worth.

The graph on the left hand side of Figure 8b illustrates the distribution of approved and booked loans from low risk A credits to extreme high risk F credits. The graph on the right hand side of Figure 8b illustrates the loss rate by risk grade over the 24 months from the date the deal was approved and booked, including the comparison to the portfolio average of 5.5%.

The graph on the left of Figure 8b shows that A graded credits account for approximately 10% of approved loans, and at the other end of the graph, F credits account for approximately 5% of the approved and booked loans. However, the graph on the right hand side of Figure 8b shows the loss rate for A credits is virtually zero while the loss rate for F credit is around 26%. In addition, the risk grades are highly correlated to the loss rate that the financial services company is experiencing. This indicates that A, B and C credits are better than average risk while E and F credits are worse than average deals. The D credits have had a loss rate that is near the portfolio average and although 4.5% might be considered high, it is significantly better than the E and F credits. Several key observations that deserve special note include the following.

The F credits represent a very unprofitable segment. It is very unlikely you can improve the deal's profitability by "pricing for the risk" or "structuring the deal" within this segment of extremely risky accounts. In addition, the F credits not only have a very high loss rate but also a very high delinquency rate, so many of these deals will be severely delinquent and will lead to future losses.

No matter what system or application process is used to underwrite deals, including a manual process using an experienced credit analyst, mistakes will be made and some losses will occur. A risk management strategy is designed to better understand the risk versus reward trade-off. A successful risk management strategy will understand the odds of success from approving the deal by risk grade and use that information to drive better decisions, resulting in higher profits.

An example of this last point is illustrated by referring to Figure 8b. While the D credits have a loss rate of approximately 4.5% it is still significantly lower than the 26% loss rate experienced with F credits. Since the loss rate of F credits is more than five times as high as the loss rate for D credits, the financial services company could approve five D credit deals for every single F credit deal rejected and still maintain the same incidence of accounts experiencing a loss. This strategy will not only lead to a higher approval rate but will also reduce the loss rate of the loans being approved and booked.

Calculating Return on Investment

The table in Figure 9 illustrates how you might calculate the Return on Investment (ROI) from implementing a risk management strategy based upon credit scoring. The table demonstrates how you would calculate the ROI impact resulting from a change in strategy from approving deals to managing a portfolio of loans. The success of the strategy is driven by adopting a portfolio approach

Figure 9: ROI Of Portfolio Strategy Based Upon One Year of Volume

Risk Grade	Old Approval Rate	New Approval Rate	Incremental Deals	Old Loss Rate	# Losses	$ Loss	Incremental Profit (2%ROA)
A	99.3%	100.0%	12	0.4%	0	$ 599	$ 3,360
B	98.4%	99.8%	94	1.3%	3	$ 18,011	$ 26,440
C	95.7%	99.0%	300	3.5%	22	$ 134,754	$ 84,069
D	83.2%	98.4%	1,517	5.0%	144	$ 864,462	$ 424,786
E	57.1%	56.7%	(43)	10.5%	(42)	$ (251,917)	$ (12,149)
F	16.1%	1.8%	(878)	26.0%	(248)	$(1,488,253)	$ (245,977)
Total	73.1%	74.9%	1,002	5.5%	(120)	$ (722,345)	$ 280,528

Calculating ROI: Total Profit Increase = ($ 722,345 + 280,528) = $1,002,873

to approving and rejecting deals. The basis of the ROI is swapping high risk E and F credits for lower risk A through D credits.

The table in Figure 9 compares the change in approval rates after applying risk grades to the deals being underwritten. The key driver of ROI is eliminating the F credits from the portfolio. Historically the financial services company was approving 16% of the F credits. This low approval rate indicates that the credit analyst realized this was a very high-risk segment. Unfortunately, even after eliminating 84% of these extremely risky deals, the ones that were approved experienced a loss rate of 26%. By rejecting extremely high-risk F credits and approving a lower percentage of very high-risk E credits, the financial services company realized a $1.75 million in reduction in loss ($1.5MM for F credits and $250K for E credits). This loss savings can now be spent by the financial services companies to buy a higher volume of A through D credits, generating more approvals.

Under this strategy, virtually all the A, B and C credits are being approved while a significantly higher percentage of D credits are approved, from 83.2% to 98.4%. Improved decisions using risk grade will permit the ability to approve better credits (A, B, C, D) and avoid unprofitable credits (E & F).

Figure 9 provides the total increase in profit possible from this enlightened strategy. The financial services company is avoiding losses from the E and F credits, resulting in 120 fewer losses. With an average loss of $6,000 per deal, this will generate a total loss savings of $722,345. Also, by approving more low-risk deals, 1,002 additional deals will be booked. Assuming a 2% return on asset (ROA), this will generate an incremental profit of $280,528 over the life of the loans approved.

The overall impact on the portfolio is an increase in approval rates from 73.1% to 74.9% and a reduction in the loss rate from 5.5% to 4.8%. The bottom line impact from one year of volume on profitability is $1,002,873, created by a reduction in loss of $722,345 and an increase in profit of $280,528 from booking more deals.

Conclusion

This chapter discusses how credit scoring has been leveraged to develop sophisticated knowledge-based decision systems. "The need for speed" has driven the rapid adoption of credit scoring within the small business lending market. Continued advances in technology and credit scoring techniques are dramatically improving the decision process for the more sophisticated lending companies. The ability to invest in advanced decision solutions is what will separate the future winners from the losers in the lending industry. The moral of the story:

"In the long run, those with the best risk strategy win."

Endnotes

[1]   For the traditional bank, an increasing competitive force has come from the "Non-bank Banks". The most prominent example of this phenomenon is the growth and power of GE Capital in today's financial markets for both consumer and commercial lending.

[2]   For more information about consumer credit scoring refer to *www.ftc.gov/bcp/conline/pubs/credit/scoring.htm.*

[3]   Within the U.S. market, there are two major commercial data bureaus, Dun & Bradstreet (D&B) and Experian Business Information Solutions (BIS). For personal or consumer data, there are three major providers, Experian, Equifax and Trans Union. These databases are compiled by gathering publicly available data, such as courthouse records, business registration, SEC data, and so forth, combined with third party provided data, primarily trade payment information.

[4]   More details can be found in V. Gerey & M. Metroka (2002, Oct.). The Future of Leasing. *Monitor: Leasing and Financial Services.*

[5]   Both D&B and Experian BIS offer generic commercial scores that are available on virtually their entire business database.

[6]   I. Fair (*www.fairisaac.com*) offers small business lending scorecards available through the LiquidCredit® Internet solution; Experian BIS offers a score specific to small business

lease financing, ~~Lease Decision Score~~™ (*www.experian.com/b2b/credit_ solutions. html*); and PredictiveMetrics, Inc. offers a Net30Score™ for accounts receivable type small business trade (*www.predictive metrics.com/index2.htm*).

[7] The major proprietors of small business custom modeling include both commercial credit bureaus (D&B and Experian), Fair Isaac (*–HYPERLINK "http://www.fico.com" — www.fairisaac.com*), and PredictiveMetrics, Inc. (*www.predictivemetrics.com*).

[8] Model maintenance involves validating the predictive power of the score compared to the original or last validation and refitting or reestimating the model if the model has shown significant deterioration.

[9] In the following, we discuss the hotly debated topic of the impact of the economic business cycle on credit scoring models' effectiveness.

[10] Some model developers exclude "indeterminates" from the model development sample; these are accounts that are neither good nor bad. Accounts pay slowly but never actually trigger the bad definition.

[11] For information related to using logistic regression for credit scoring, see M. Banasiak & D. Tantum (1999). Accurately and efficiently measuring individual account credit risk on existing portfolios. *The Credit and Financial Management Review,* 5(1). More technical information about Logist Regression can be found in J. H. Aldrich & F.D. Nelson (1984). Linear Probability, Logit and Probit Models. *Sage University Papers: Quantitative applications in the social sciences,* 07-45, Beverly Hills, CA: Sage; and R. S. Pindyck & D.L. Rubinfeld, *Econometric Models and Economic Forecasts. McGraw* Hill, Inc.

12   A more comprehensive discussion of reject inference for small business credit scoring model development can be found in D. Tantum (2003). *Reject inference: The art of new application model development.* White Paper. PredictiveMetrics Inc.

13   In the U.S., the external commercial bureau data used are typically from D&B and Experian BIS.

14   The use of consumer bureau data for credit underwriting is highly regulated in the United States by the Fair Credit Reporting Act (FCRA). For details on the use of consumer credit data for commercial lending within the FCRA guidelines see www.ftc.gov/os/statutes/fcra.htm.

15   For example, credit scores may range between 1-100 or 250-850, with the probability of a bad rating being higher for lower scores and decreasing as the score increases. In most cases the score is calibrated such that a fixed incremental change in score causes the good to bad odds ratio to change by a fixed amount. For example, it is common for a score increase of 20 points to be calibrated to a doubling of the good to bad rating odds.

Editor's Notes

The preceding chapter rounds out our applications of data mining and quantitative analysis techniques that are prevalent in the financial lending industry. It extends off Chapter 2 by providing a more detailed look at how lending organizations utilize these techniques in order to more effectively manage risk while also reducing the time of the decision making process in lending to small businesses. Through the combination of relevant data, appropriate modeling techniques and sound business strategy, lending organizations can better manage the new customer acquisition process along with more effectively managing the risk of current borrowers, which can ultimately enhance their overall performance and profitability. Our next section will turn to how data mining and business intelligence can help enhance the highly complex business process of customer relationship management within the insurance and consumer products industry.

Chapter IV

The Utilization of Business Intelligence and Data Mining in the Insurance Marketplace

Jeff Hoffman

The Chubb Group of Insurance Companies, USA

Introduction

NASA Missions are as varied as the mandate of the agency. From using satellite imaging to study climate change to scanning deep space with the Hubble Space Telescope, NASA's primary goal is to further humankind's knowledge of our universe.

Pioneering the future. Pushing the envelope. Just as NASA's goals stretch our thoughts, business intelligence (BI) and data mining take us on a journey that continuously provides discovery of new and valuable information, giving us insight into the unknown.

Customers, products and markets are our galaxy, BI and data mining technology are our Apollo rockets and space shuttles, and our greatest asset, the excellence of the people at the helm of the technology, are our astronauts. It is about creating the future.

Exploration using business intelligence and data mining can teach us to view our businesses in a brand new way.

About Chubb & Son

In 1882, Thomas Caldecot Chubb and his son Percy opened their marine underwriting business in the seaport district of New York City. They focused on insuring ships and cargo. Over time, the company branched out into commercial property and casualty insurance and personal insurance as well. The Chubb Corporation was formed in 1967 and was listed on the New York Stock Exchange in 1984. It now ranks among the top 10 publicly traded insurance organizations based on revenues in the United States. With more than 13,000 employees throughout North America, Europe, South America, and the Pacific Rim, Chubb serves property and casualty customers from more than 130 offices in 31 countries. Chubb works closely with 8,000 independent agents and brokers worldwide.

Chubb is a leading provider of a broad range of standard and specialty property and liability insurance products and services to businesses, not-for-profit organizations and individuals. Chubb offers world-class services including claim handling and loss control as well as e-commerce solutions.

As a company, Chubb has never tried to be all things to all people, and never strived to be the biggest insurer in the world. Instead, Chubb has always concentrated on serving businesses and individuals that need more than conventional or 'generic' insurance. In personal insurance, Chubb focuses on creating policies for individuals who have sophisticated insurance needs. The insurer serves clients who own fine homes, automobiles, watercraft, art, antiques and collectibles. In commercial insurance, Chubb is known for companies in the high-tech, life science and energy industries, as well as banks, law firms and many other businesses. Its world-wide network enables it to effectively respond to the insurance and risk management needs of multinational companies.

Chubb has always been known for its service to policyholders — especially paying claims in an expedient and fair manner. The company consistently receives high ratings from A.M. Best Company for financial stability and from Standard & Poor's and Moody's for its claims-paying ability.

Cost-Effective Revenue Growth — Targeted Customer Acquisition

The application of business intelligence and data mining within the marketing and sales arena can yield very favorable results. It should be developed as a core competency that supports the delivery and *strategic* use of consistent, accurate and meaningful information throughout the enterprise. The marketing and sales functions discussed here will focus specifically on customer acqui-sition, a key component to customer relationship management.

Chubb relies on its vast independent agency network to dis-tribute and sell its products and services. These 8,000 agents and brokers are not captive to Chubb and can offer several options to clients when placing their insurance. Therefore, Chubb and other insurance carriers must consider this dynamic when developing new or executing existing acquisition strategies.

Selling additional products to current customers or increasing coverage on their current purchases provides a large opportunity for Chubb. With many different product and coverage offerings available throughout its personal, commercial and specialty operations, Chubb-appointed agents have a diverse inventory to offer their clients. Many of these clients begin their insurance relationship with Chubb by purchasing one or two coverages. Relationship building with the agent and client over time is of great importance and can take the form of several different types of interactions.

The underwriting and service staff at the point of sale offer the agent and insurance buyer expertise that is considered near or at the top of the industry. A commercial client may experience the technical assessment of a loss control specialist who can help a risk manager develop and implement workplace safety and other risk management programs. Another commercial customer may have specialty insurance needs. Its people may interact with a Chubb underwriter who has a deep understanding of employment practices liability and can articulate significant exposures that have not been considered. A personal client who owns a collection of unique lithographs may have the opportunity to work with one of Chubb's fine art appraisers who will help ensure that coverage limits reflect values. After being exposed to Chubb's expertise and capabilities, clients realize that the insurer takes the time to deeply understand their insurance and risk management needs and can provide service beyond offering a wide range of coverages.

For Chubb, the main objectives associated with utilizing business intelligence and data mining in relation to sales and marketing are to increase revenue while reducing the cost of acquisition and retaining valuable customers. The goal is to serve up actionable intelligence information that allows people to use their time and resources in the most efficient way possible.

There are four steps that are required to achieve a customer acquisition continuum that will yield significant results for sales and marketing. Lead qualification, prospect management, results analy-

Figure 1: The Customer Acquisition Continuum

The objective is to serve up actionable intelligence information that allows a firm to use its time and resources in the most efficient way possible

sis, and lead refinement are all critical and need to be implemented and sustained with as much discipline and accountability as are given to the underwriting and claim operations (see Figure 1).

Due to the immense size of Chubb's independent agency network, it is difficult to ensure that each producer in every agent's and broker's office maintains a deep knowledge of Chubb products, coverage options and underwriting appetite. This situation leads to agents submitting business to Chubb for clients who may not agree with the price/value associated with Chubb's offerings. Keeping careful watch over resource capacity, it is important for Chubb's human resources to expend its efforts pricing and underwriting those accounts that have the highest propensity to purchase coverage.

Are all current customers a target for cross-sell or up-sell? How does a firm determine which customers to offer additional products or coverage to? What are the characteristics of prospective clients that have yet to purchase? The *lead qualification* process should begin with taking inventory of the current customer base. Gaining insight into current customers who have already perceived value in an organization's offerings can lead to additional sales with those clients and assist in developing profiles of prospects that have yet to buy.

There are four measures that are extremely important in qualifying customers for cross-sell and up-sell — determining a customer's current relative value to the organization, segmenting or grouping customers with other customers who look and behave similarly, uncovering how likely or unlikely a customer is to purchase a specific product or coverage and identifying the intermediaries that are most effective at selling. The end game is to *target the right customers with the right products via the most effective distribution channel.*

Once leads are qualified and distributed to the optimal channel, providing agents with the appropriate collateral to help them make a sale, following up on their progress with the client and tracking the activity within the sales process is critical. Qualifying leads pinpoints the target, but *managing prospects with the individual at the point of sale is what will make or break the result.* By providing targeted leads and spending time to follow up with agents on individual prospects, you shift the sales and marketing activity from reactionary to proactive. This forces a stronger and trusted relationship with the agency and can lead to additional new business sourced by that agent with the Chubb offering in mind.

Any new business written, whether it comes in the form of selling additional products to existing customers or by acquiring new ones, should include careful analysis of the intermediary making the sale. An important component to prospecting is profiling and assessing the effectiveness of the sales. This exercise should include two areas of focus. The first evaluates the financial and productivity results of the sales organization. The other examines their knowledge and expertise relative to specific coverages and customer segments. Financial variables measured can reveal a great deal about the type of client they are selling to and their amount of commitment to producing new business. Additional variables can identify a sales organization's expertise in placing business with clients based upon their industry, demographics or size and determine how well they understand which potential customers will see value in a specific product offering. All of these measures should be evaluated in conjunction with one another and need to be appropriately weighted according to the business strategy being implemented at that time. This multivariable approach produces a comprehensive and objective methodology that brings consistency to the process regardless of geographic or size differences.

Working with an independent agent, who is working within his or her own workflow and systems, forces the Chubb staff in the local office to record the progress being made with each qualified prospect developed. Which prospects are distributed to which agents? How many contacts have been made with an agent relative to a specific prospect? Did we provide a quote? Did Chubb have any direct contact with the prospect? Did we eliminate the prospect and if so, for what reason? Was the agent successful in selling a policy to the prospect? The tools and the discipline to capture this information is important in measuring Chubb's performance relative to prospecting.

Prospecting activities require oversight that differs greatly from the more standard audits that take place for profitability, growth and new customer goals. This oversight must measure, recognize and reward people differently and in order to do that, *specific types of information detailing the sales process need to be available.* Examples of these measures are:

- Measuring how many prospects are in an individual's branch office or zone sales pipeline at any given time.
- Outlining the duration and how far into the sales cycle prospects were pursued (i.e., a prospect was given to a producer and quoted, but then eliminated due to pricing four months after first contact was made).
- Capturing how much revenue was generated through the sales pipeline for a given period of time.
- Analyzing prospect removal reasons to identify "inability to close" issues.

There are additional *analyses that assist management with setting the ongoing strategic direction associated with prospecting.* These provide current and projected figures that measure changes relative to the cost of acquisition. These include various hit ratios that describe the efficiency of the prospecting process.

The effectiveness of lead qualification is measured by analyzing the ratio of prospects distributed to the number of policies written. This ratio can reveal whether the lead qualifiers are being optimally applied when targeting a prospect group. It can also identify weaknesses related to the qualifiers themselves. Either way, consistent use of the information that is used to develop the leads must be "field tested" and stay intact for at least 18 months in order to prove or disprove its effectiveness. The reason for this is that the insurance sales cycle can last for many months and it may take at least a full renewal period for a client to understand what is being offered and appropriately budget for the new product or coverage. For each prospect created, the specific qualifiers used should be captured and compared to the prospect status to determine which qualifiers yield the best results.

Many prospects are eliminated at different points in the sales process. Understanding the overall percentage that are eliminated and the reason they were eliminated in relation to the number of leads generated gives a firm deeper insight into the factors contributing to not making a sale. Was price a factor? Did the agent have enough expertise selling a specific product or coverage? These factors may or may not be considered when qualifying prospects, but *careful analysis of the reasons for not closing a deal can lead to future enhancements to the qualification process that will continuously improve close rates.*

Targeted customer acquisition seems simple on the surface. Many business people profess to know and understand their customers and the marketplace well enough that they feel the investments required to develop leads, manage prospects, measure results and refine the process are not needed to succeed. What needs to be answered, however, is whether they are conducting these activities in the most cost-effective manner and obtaining more consistent results.

Are the people at the point of sale spending their time developing and sustaining relationships with agents and working on closing new business *or* are they tied to their desks attempting to gather the right information from several different sources to figure out which clients to target and which agents to approach with these targets? Is management learning about what drives sales by analyzing the key aspects of the sales cycle? Do we understand which customers are driving profitability and how their profile differs from those that do not? The answers to these very important questions are examples of some of the critical drivers that can produce significantly better results when looking at activities surrounding the acquisition of new customers.

Applying Business Intelligence and Data Mining to Enhance the Customer Acquisition Process

Getting closer to the customer. Learning more about their needs. Determining their value to the organization. All are common mantras vocalized by consultants at every turn and discussed as important activities within the walls of most firms today. All are important and require organizations to obtain data and information. What really matters is how to optimally apply the information. Within the customer acquisition process, business intelligence and data mining can be applied along the way to share these and other insights in a format in which swift action can be taken by the information consumer.

Within the customer acquisition process, BI and data mining are applied in the following ways:

- To differentiate and value customers and distribution partners
- To determine the likelihood that a customer will purchase a specific offering
- To offer the right product to the right customer via the right channel
- To measure sales activity and performance over time

Customer Differentiation

Customer differentiation is at the heart of an organization's acquisition and retention efforts. Multiple techniques can be applied to describe the similarities and differences among customers. There are specific techniques that work best when the goal is targeting prospects as new customers.

The ability to identify prospects that will ultimately bring value to the organization relies heavily upon clustering, an undirected form of segmentation. This is an exploratory data analysis (EDA) technique used to dissect a heterogeneous collection of data into a manageable number of homogenous (or *natural*) subgroups. This will group customers that possess similar characteristics and clearly describe why one group is different from another. The basic goal here is to find those future clients that look and act very much like current valuable ones. Careful analysis of the current customer base is conducted that includes the use of data collected through the insurance interaction. The first step is to determine the targeted market. This exercise may take the form of either simply choosing an already known customer group that is being targeted for increased penetration or may consist of market analysis that identifies an opportunistic segment. Once the target is chosen, depending upon the size and makeup of the population, *multiple iterations of clustering* are conducted to determine a customer set that is optimal. This multilayered clustering method can apply only if there are enough records in any given cluster to make the results statistically significant. There are varying opinions on just how large that number is, but experiences seem to set the bar at 300 customer records per segment. Once complete, these "newly discovered" segments of customers should be valued in a way that will *prioritize one group over the next*. Profiles of each of these prioritized groups are then developed utilizing only third party data and this then forms the basis for targeting the sales effort.

The development of a *Customer Value Index (CVI)*, or weighted variable that scores each customer record and rank orders them relative to one another, is a directed form of segmentation that utilizes business knowledge and experience to drive its results. The CVI measures a customer's current value to the organization based upon selected underwriting criteria. It is not a predictor of future value, nor does it provide measurement for lifetime value. The output of the CVI calculation is a score that is then distributed into percentile groups. These groups are then translated to customer value tiers (i.e., Platinum, Gold, Silver, etc.), which are then used to *differentiate service levels, develop profiles for prospecting or prioritize cross-sell activity.*

Example CVI Calculation

- CVI is derived from X number of weighted components (a number agreed upon by business managers who have the most exposure to the client group being assessed). Each customer receives a rating for each component based on criteria such as that defined below. The CVI value levels will be determined by adding the weighted scores for each component and placing them in X number of categories based on a XX% split top to bottom. Value level labels are then assigned: that is, Platinum, Gold, Silver, Bronze and Standard. For example, the customers' scores that fall in the top XX% will be labeled Platinum, the next XX% will be Gold, and so forth. The following is an example of how a CVI would be developed:

Example Customer Value Index (CVI) calculation:
- Five Components of CVI:
  1. Measurement of a customer's contribution of revenue
  2. Customer Tenure
  3. Customer Risk Rating
  4. Geography

5. Share of Wallet — Number of products currently pur-
    chased
- Weight of each Component:
    1. Customer Revenue contribution   .20
    2. Customer Tenure   .15
    3. Risk Rating   .20
    4. Geography   .15
    5. Share of Wallet   .30

- *Component Rating* — combination of one rating from Customer Size, one rating from Customer Tenure, one rating from
  Risk Rating, one rating from Geography and a combined rating
  of applicable types of coverage for Share of Wallet.

  For example, ABC Corp. contributes $280,000 in annual
  revenue with a rating of 10, has been a customer for six years,
  holds a risk rating of 8, is headquartered in New Jersey with
  a rating of 3 and has purchased Coverage A, Coverage B and
  three coverages from Product Z. ABC's CVI score would be
  $6.9 = [(10*.2) + (6*.15) + (8*.2) + (6*.15) + (10/2*.3)]$.
  Let's assume that this customer falls between the top 25th to
  30th percentile and that there are five desired customer value
  levels. A score of 6.9 would hypothetically place ABC Corp.
  in the Gold value level.

Using the undirected and directed segmentation techniques
described here in conjunction with one another supplies a more
precise view of customer groups and provides insight into those
that bring the most value to the organization. The same techniques
are then applied to distribution partners to set the stage for
developing effective sales programs. Profiles of targeted prospects are developed and matched to intelligence information about

agents and brokers who have historically displayed their experience working with clients with similar characteristics.

Purchase Propensity

Given the *current* customer base for product *x*, *who* will *most likely* become purchasers of product *x*? This question is answered by providing *portfolio assessment* capabilities vs. one-over-one account handling. Statistical modeling and data mining algorithms in conjunction with a database or file that can include internal data about a customer's relationships and interactions, and derived data that identify the customer's value to the firm and its similarities or differences from other customers are applied.

This process of model development is *iterative*. Several models using different flavors of techniques are developed (additional information about this process will be outlined later). The models are assessed for their predictability strength relative to the modeling outcome desired. Each customer is designated a score that rank orders his or her propensity to purchase relative to another. The output of the models are usually interpreted as if-then-else statements that describe, in terms of the data and their values, reasons that one customer may be more likely to purchase than another.

Using purchase propensity data within the customer acquisition process creates a more effective sales result. A *marketing lift chart* displays an example of this effect. The lift chart plots two lines against two axes, one showing the percentage of customers marketed to, the other the percentage of responses to that marketing effort. The first line explains what will happen if no purchase propensity data are used within the sales and marketing effort. The second line explains the lift that can be realized by utilizing purchase propensity data. This shows that a smaller percentage of customers need to be accessed in order to achieve the same percentage of responses when using such techniques. The obvious benefit is that in the end, marketers are focusing their efforts first on those prospects that will yield the most favorable outcome.

Linking Customers and Distribution

Targeting customers is half the battle. Determining the best way to access those customers is the next step. Combining the derived information about agents' and brokers' strengths and value to the organization with a stable of qualified prospects guides the effort of the all-important linkage to the most effective distribution. The right agents or brokers are not those who have large lists of current customers who have not yet purchased. They are those who have proven they can sell the types of coverage to those prospects that have been identified as most likely to purchase. Business intelligence platforms are developed that make it easy for marketing managers to access this information and distribute leads with minimal work effort. This efficient platform frees up time for the marketers to work closely with agents and brokers to help sell and close new business.

Tracking the sales process, once leads are distributed, is key in determining whether the BI and data mining efforts are working. Tracking contact with customers, identifying success in moving them closer to a purchase (i.e., indicating or securing a quote), eliminating a prospect and successfully closing a deal provide important prospect management information, which is then fed back into the customer and distribution profiling and modeling efforts to continually improve the ongoing sales and marketing efforts.

Measuring Performance

There are two aspects to performance measurement that are supported by business intelligence. The first is assessing the operational activity and success associated with customer acquisition. This activity includes day-to-day analysis of prospects in the sales pipeline at different points and can supply the local marketer with important information about the effectiveness of their distribution partners. The second aspect of performance measurement is related to intelligence information that can be derived from sales activity. This intelligence supplies management with aggregated information that is used to drive future strategies related to the sales and marketing function. In either case, data is cleansed, consolidated and delivered via decision support tools that enable optimal flexibility for the user and serve refreshed information in a timely manner to the right people (see Figure 2).

Figure 2: Obtaining the Right Customers

Before BI and Data Mining	With BI and Data Mining
- Utilized Internal Chubb purchaser data	- Uses combination of internal, and derived data
- Lists of Non-buyers	- Qualified Leads
- Focused on Agents with large lists and good relationships	- Targets Agents that have proven they can sell
- Casts a wide net	- Pinpoint prospects
- Low hit ratio	- Improved hit ratio
- High cost of Acquisition	- Decreased cost of Acquisition

Using state-of-the-art tools and techniques to drive cost effective growth

Developing a Business Intelligence Platform and Data Mining Solutions

Investment in a business intelligence capability or data mining solution is a strategic decision that should be made as either a *prerequisite to the business planning process* or as *a component of the business plan* to support a specific goal. The business planning process should be conducted with as much insight about customers, distribution, products and competition as possible. BI and data mining can contribute greatly to this by identifying opportunities and weaknesses in the business that on the surface may not be obvious. As a component of the business plan, decisions to invest in certain key areas of infrastructure are also made. The business plan, for example, may outline a focus on the development of a disciplined prospecting process, such as the one noted earlier. Business intelligence and data mining can be the backbone to this infrastructure by providing the tools needed to support lead qualification, prospect management and results measurement.

Regardless of how and where BI and data mining capabilities are targeted, the processes to develop them are the same. There are six steps required:

- Business discovery
- Data analysis
- Data preparation
- Modeling
- Database design
- Platform development

Business discovery typically takes the form of small workshops or several one-on-one interviews. Sessions are facilitated with the objective to draw out specific informational requirements from individuals who will become the consumer of the intelligence. As an example, if the target is providing improved decision-making with respect to retention activities, the discussion will be geared toward the current process and what is deemed important when considering if a customer should be retained or not. This exercise will identify pertinent data variables that will be considered "high priority" when developing the file or files for analysis. The business discovery process should include documentation that specifies the objectives and scope of effort, detailed data requirements (including external and derived data specifications), functionality required (if platform development is needed), user group(s) targeted and workflow and process maps that will outline the optimal use of the new intelligence information by the end user.

The data analysis effort begins by investigating databases for candidate sources of the data needed. Optimal sources are selected by analyzing data variables for:

- Population frequency
- Range of values
- Data translation (presence of code table documentation)

Once the data source analysis is complete, variable selection can be conducted. This includes an exercise that assesses the hygiene of each variable in relation to the next. If there are key variables required for the initiative whose quality of data is in question, a decision may be made to either have this data populated with "default" values that reflect "average" response for the population as a whole or be completely eliminated. This data quality analysis can lead to source transactional data system enhancements that focus on the improvement of data entry workflow and/or system edits that can improve the overall quality of data within the organization.

Data acquisition is the next step in the process. Writing detailed specifications for data extraction is first completed. These specifications guide the programming resources in their efforts to extract the required data variables. *Extraction, transformation and load (ETL) software should be utilized to build the extract programs to ensure the presence of speed, consistency and documentation.* The ETL process consolidates and transforms all of the data variables from the various source extracts and then loads the result into a "signature" file. A signature file is one that contains records with all pertinent variables present per record. An example of this is a "customer signature" file that contains all data variables needed for each customer. This file can then be used as input to analysis and modeling activity such as customer value measurement, segmentation or purchase propensity modeling.

Once the signature file is created, model development can begin. Model development is a process that includes the creation and evaluation of several models. Each model may utilize a different technique (i.e., linear regression, decision tree, rule induction, etc.) and the models' performance is measured in relation to one another and the targeted business objective. Models are trained using an iterative process that uses goodness-of-fit statistics to differentiate the challengers from the champion. Using a purchase propensity model as an example, model training begins with a snapshot of *known* purchasers (assigned a value of 1) and non-purchasers (assigned a value of 0). A sample is designed for model *training;*

Figure 3

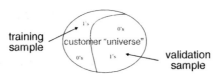

another sample is set aside to *validate* resultant models (see Figure 3).

Lift charts, or 2-D and 3-D representations of *scored valida-tion data* sorted by purchase likelihood are created. The vertical axis denotes *% purchasers,* while the horizontal axis denotes *decile groups.* The area between lift chart curves is the *gain* delivered by model usage versus non-targeted execution (see Figure 4).

Diagnostic classification charts are produced to highlight *agree-ment* between *predicted* purchasers and *actual* purchasers and *predicted* non-purchasers and *actual* non-purchasers.

Confidence in the model or models developed leads to the design and development of a database that incorporates both internal and derived variables. This repository, or data mart, is the backbone to enable the end user to take action against the intelli-

Figure 4: Measures of Model Predictive Power

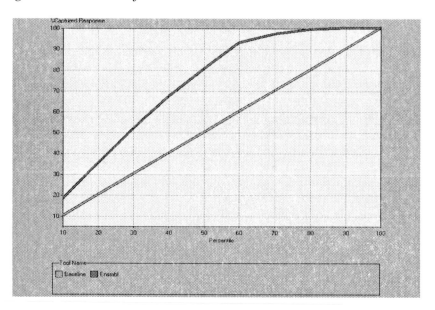

gence being delivered. The data mart essentially incorporates the model results into a usable format.

On top of this data mart should sit a decision support platform that releases the power of the underlying data to the end user. There are many software packages available today that can support decision support analysis. This analysis capability should enable multiple variables to be scrutinized against one another and should support the ability to drill-down to further detail on those data variables that warrant it. There should exist flexibility within the package to customize views of data efficiently in order to support several different business intelligence platforms throughout the firm.

BI and Data Mining – Impact on the Organization

Business intelligence and data mining can have significant impact on an organization; some positive, some negative. The positive impact can be measured in terms of *operational efficiency,* which can be realized in relatively short order. *Improved decision-making* has more of a long-term and sustainable impact within the organization, as it feeds strategic choices made about customer, distribution, product and service strategies. The negative impact BI and data mining can have is related to the potential misuse of the new information made available. People's jobs may change. They may be accountable for new activities that could force them to behave differently. The incentives that drive people's performance may no longer be commensurate to what may be expected of them in the future. If these changes are not identified and addressed before deployment of new BI platforms, the ROI targeted will not be achieved.

At Chubb, BI and data mining have surfaced improvements in a number of areas. Account management is an area in which new and improved customer data enable historic analysis of a customer's relationship with the firm. The development of risk qualification models has enabled the triage of risks prior to performing a complete underwriting assessment. This serves to focus the attention on those accounts that warrant it. A reduction in the cost of acquisition of new customers has been realized by creating a lead qualification platform that assists in targeting those customers that are most likely to purchase from Chubb. Chubb's relationship with its agents and brokers has therefore been strengthened. It is easier to describe the Chubb appetite, which helps the agent to understand the profile of the type of customer to offer Chubb coverage to. Over time, the trust and confidence that an agent has with Chubb increases, which can lead to increased revenue and improved retention. The power of the data consolidation, data cleansing and analysis capabilities that accompany business intelligence has improved Chubb's ability to more deeply understand its overall enterprise exposures. Chubb may protect a customer's risks across several different areas of its business. These are considered exposures to Chubb and need careful attention and oversight. BI has been the backbone in creating this important analysis utility. The expectation that intelligence information within the organization and a discipline to use it are present is an underlying positive impact that BI and data mining have surfaced at Chubb. It is viewed as a core competency and relevant component of infrastructure that is considered strategic and tactical alike. With its presence, individuals are expected to change their mindset from being reactive to proactive and as such, business models and technology platforms must allow for maximum flexibility.

The surfacing of new ideas within a firm is an asset that is required in today's business environment if long-term sustainable earnings growth is to be attained. BI and data mining is helping Chubb to become a learning organization that fosters such thought. The potential impact realized can be great, but for Chubb and many other firms like it, the journey has just begun.

How Data Mining Fits Into the Overall Organizational Strategy

Chubb is a company that has been around for over a century and prides itself on its integrity, management discipline and exper-tise. Data mining is a unique science that provides insightful infor-mation to Chubb's human resources, enabling thoughtful decision-making that touches our customers and agents everyday and provides ongoing value to our shareholders. Offering specialized products and services at a competitive price to clients and execut-ing with optimal operating efficiency are strategies that are consis-tent throughout the enterprise. Data mining and business intelli-gence support these strategies by unlocking data about customers, agents, products and competitors and through algorithmic pattern recognition, serve new business insights to underwriters, claim staff and managers every day.

All data mining and business intelligence development is centered within Chubb's Strategic Marketing Department. Teams of experts work with business managers from Chubb's Strategic Business Units, marrying process and technique with relevant subject matter knowledge and business experience. The key asset, the individuals within Strategic Marketing, work with a proven methodology that allows them to deliver solutions quickly to internal business partners that are not only focused on intelligence data, but also address change associated with their use.

Creating Business Opportunities in the Future with Business Intelligence and Data Mining

"Libraries are loaded with information, most of it free. Intelligence costs money, because it's about time rather than information."[1] The competitive advantage that a solid business intelligence platform can bring to an enterprise relies on speed. When an organization *gains access to pertinent information quickly*, and *synthesizes it effectively*, intelligence is created that can be acted upon to optimize customer value and lead to increased earnings.

The future of business intelligence and data mining in a business setting will become more and more important. Organizations today are just beginning to realize value from investing in these technologies and techniques. The business intuition and experience of people will remain the most important asset, but receiving improved, more complete information quickly and linking it to the workflows and processes that support better decision-making can give a firm competitive advantage in the future.

Passive vs. Active Intelligence

It is important to recognize the distinction between passive and active intelligence. Passive intelligence, the most widely used today, relies on people to take action on the information put before them. They can either act or not. Active intelligence is the utilization of informational data networking to drive automated actions. A system that includes active intelligence is designed and constructed to always take action when data instruct it to. An example of this would be within a Web service portal for customers. It would start by identifying a visitor as a "high value" customer through the integration of business intelligence data derived and stored in a customer relationship management database. Depending upon the path that this customer takes in the service portal, specific product or service offerings may be dynamically presented to them if they have a high purchase propensity score present. Another example would be to utilize data derived via data mining to automatically "tier" service for clients. Differentiating a high value versus low value customer can drive high-touch/low-touch service solutions and move overall expenses to a level that is commensurate to what a customer expects and how an organization values its clients.

Mining of Unstructured Data

Mining of unstructured data is a relatively new and untested technique, but may still be quite valuable to organizations in the future. There are algorithms being developed and already available in the marketplace that can recognize patterns within narrative or textual format. Not many organizations have implemented this advanced data mining technique as of yet due to mixed results regarding the algorithms' ability to consistently identify similar patterns. This is due in part to the processes used to parse text accurately and create structured data variables from unstructured strings. If and when this technology matures, there will be many important applications for it within businesses in the future. An example within the property and casualty insurance industry would be to mine an aggregated group of loss description narratives to identify patterns describing common situations that lead to certain size, complexity or duration of a claim settlement. Further analysis of these patterns could also uncover data that are predictive of fraudulent activity.

Business intelligence and the use of data mining differs greatly from traditional reporting in that it is not only delivering the answer to the "what" question, but more importantly, the "why", as it identifies statistically significant data variables that drive certain performance. Understanding how to provide this intelligence in the right places within the organization in the future will spell the difference between short-term success and sustaining competitive advantage over time.

Endnotes

[1]   Baker, J.S., Jr., Friedman, G., Friedman, M., & Chapman, C. (1997). *The intelligence edge.* New York: Crown Publishers, Inc.

Editor's Notes

The process of enhancing the strategic initiative of customer relationship management is no doubt an essential topic to companies across industry sectors. One way to achieve efficiencies in this complex area is through the combination of data, technology and "smart" management. In this past chapter, Chubb Ins. clearly illustrated this concept in describing its activities in leveraging available data with the various components of business intelligence technology in conjunction with sound management strategy to increase the efficiency of better servicing the market in which it operates. A vital component of this process was to enhance its functional activities with its existing sales force network. The following chapter will further address the concept of driving CRM, this time in the consumer products industry, also by the utilization of data mining to enhance sales force management tactics.

Chapter V

Sales Force Management in the Consumer Products Industry

Navin Sharma, PhD
Marketwell Inc., USA

Introduction

One of the largest direct-selling companies in the world, with sales forces in the U.S. and abroad, sells a line of beauty, health, and fitness products through a network of independent sales representatives. Currently in the United States alone, the representative population has grown to several hundred thousand individuals. Representatives purchase products from the company at a discount, and in turn, sell them to their own customers, earning revenue through volume discounts. Customers order their products from catalogs that contain a mix of seasonally appropriate items along with core and new products, and special promotions to choose from. To assist its field sales force, this consumer products organization provides incentives, sales recognition awards, and training programs in beauty consultation and sales effectiveness.

Given such a large and varied sales force, the potential of experiencing significant sales-rep turnover exists. As a result, the company needs to target its sales and marketing efforts for maximum sales effectiveness. One of the targeting measures currently being evaluated is *lifetime value:* the expected value of a representative for the length of the representative's tenure.

One of the principles of direct marketing is that it generally costs less to keep an existing customer than to acquire a new one. This is also applicable to sales representatives, as the costs associated with advertising for new representatives, meeting with and evaluating prospects, and training new hires can be substantial compared with the costs associated with efforts to retain current representatives. An early warning system that identifies representatives who are at risk of attrition, along with an assessment of their future value, would support a retention program that targets the most profitable customers from among the "at risk" population.

Concept of Lifetime Value

How can we identify our best customers? Many companies use a measure of *lifetime value* (LTV) for a customer. LTV is an estimate of the total revenue generated by a customer over the entire duration of the customer relationship. It is generally measured in terms of gross sales, although total profit, when available, can be a more accurate measure.

Lifetime value for a sales-rep is a projection, or forecast, of the future sales produced by a representative from the measurement date forward. In particular, we are interested in the performance of new representatives, which refers to those who have been with the company for less than four months. In the early stages of a representative's tenure, the company has very little to go by in evaluating a representative's potential: this is the period of maximum attrition and risk for the company. A reliable projection of "future value" will help guide training, incentive, and marketing efforts, producing a better return on investment in these areas.

Lifetime value models actually provide useful information at two "poles": At the high end, they identify the most profitable representatives to target and at the low end, they identify the least profitable representatives, whose resources allocated may be reduced accordingly.

For our purposes, a practical definition of lifetime value is: the sum total of net operational sales for a representative for the next year:

Lifetime Value is the sum of Total Sales, or Net Revenue to the company, for the next 12 months.

Benefits of the LTV Measure

The LTV approach provides a number of strategic benefits when considering the performance of representatives, which involve the following:

- It focuses on the "total" value of a representative, not just the sales he/she generates in a particular month or campaign.
- It projects a representative's future potential, and is more appropriate for planning and strategy than measures of past performance.

- It can be used to create representative segments. Segments with different characteristics can be managed selectively.
- It can be used in financial analysis, to estimate ROI and break-even points for strategies.

Practical Application of Lifetime Value

The LTV method can help streamline organizational operations. More specifically, it can:

- Measure the success of ongoing sales and marketing strategies.
- Identify representative characteristics useful for recruitment, retention, and revenue growth programs.
- Customer relationship management: mailings and outbound calling programs based on lifetime value scores and segments for sales growth and retention objectives.
- Generate overall business indicators to compare past performance, and to project future company sales.

Development of a Lifetime Value Measure

To develop a model to estimate LTV we apply multiple regression techniques. With this methodology we developed models for predicting a representative's lifetime value based on available representative information.

We utilized several sources of information for the models, which included (see Figure 1):

- Representative characteristics: age, credit indicators, and the results of a personal interview preceding appointment;
- Census characteristics of the district: income and wealth

Figure 1

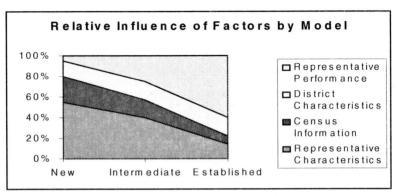

indicators, family composition and other population characteristics;

- Characteristics of the representative's sales region: field measures of past sales, sales growth, and staff composition;
- Operational performance measures, such as past sales and
  activity.

Our modeling exercise revealed that we could achieve a
balance between accuracy and complexity by generating three
models, based on the length of the customer relationship:

- *Model 1:* For a brand new representative, initial contact
  information and census data provide the building blocks for
  the model.
- *Model 2:* When a representative has been with the company
  for more than two months, internally generated data about the
  customer relationship are much more important than initial
  contact information or census data. Not surprisingly, the
  model for "established" representatives is the most accurate.
- *Model 3:* For representatives with limited history, an intermediate model using all data sources works best, as we transition

Figure 2

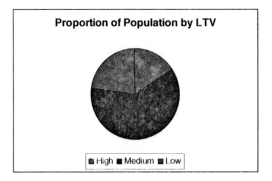

from little knowledge to a lot of knowledge about the customer.

Lifetime value scoring provides a means for segmenting new representatives. We consider three segments as an example (segments could be further refined if needed):

- We define a "high performer" segment for the top 16% of new representatives in terms of lifetime value. This cutoff is based on our experience with the overall population of representatives, in which approximately 16% consistently surpass annual sales targets set by management.
- A significant proportion of representatives have $0 predicted lifetime value. These are representatives from whom we will get no further sales, and who will either leave or be removed in the near future. We will call this segment "attrition representatives".
- The remaining representatives are "average performers", falling in between the two extremes.

These are typical results for segmentation models based on lifetime value. Note that we can identify significant subpopulations for both "positive" actions — high LTV, and "negative" actions: low LTV. In general, resources can be shifted away from low LTV representatives towards high LTV representatives.

Model Accuracy: Gains Chart

So far, the results we have presented are those of a predictive, statistical model. While the model points to the possibility of identifying, say, a high performer subpopulation, we need to determine its accuracy in actually identifying the right people. In other words, while the model identifies a particular group of representatives as being among the top 16% of LTV scores, in reality, some of them will turn out to perform at the medium or low LTV level. Conversely, some representatives with low to medium predicted LTV will actually perform at the high LTV level. To evaluate the model, we compare actual versus predicted LTV scores on a validation sample. A gains chart/plot (Figure 3) helps to demonstrate the accuracy of the model. This plot shows (once

Figure 3

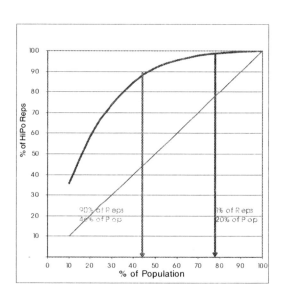

we rank representatives by predicted LTV) how much of the population that we have to cover in order to capture 90% of representatives who actually achieved a high LTV status.

Figure 3 shows that, in order to actually reach 90% of the top 16% of representatives, we would have to contact 48% of the representative population. Note another important finding: if we eliminate the bottom 20% of the population as scored by the model, we would miss only 1% of the top performers! Depending on our objectives, either "tail" of the scored population could be useful for targeting strategies.

Applications: Lifetime Value as a Field Management Tool

As previously mentioned, LTV can help streamline operational activities and enhance strategic management initiatives. The following section provides an example of this.

Lifetime value scores and segments could be available to sales managers as an aid to decision-making and management.

Field managers could assess the state of the new representative population to determine:

- Which representatives show potential, and deserve extra help;
- Among representatives who are about to leave, who among them might merit special retention efforts based on lifetime value potential;
- Planning for recruitment efforts based on current attrition potential; and
- Expected performance of the sales region relative to the prior year, and to other regions.

Samples from two hypothetical sales districts demonstrate the kind of information that could be provided.

Applications: Lifetime Value for Customer Relationship Management

Customer service is an important element in this organization's sales support strategy. The company runs its own call center to address representative inquiries, update and add to orders, and makes adjustments to a representative's account as necessary. The call centers field more than 1 million calls a month. In managing the flow of calls, lifetime value can be applied to prioritize and direct calls. A representative is required to enter his/her account number, which allows the system to look up his/her lifetime value. Operational activities can be adjusted in the following ways:

- Call center agents can be matched with representatives: Experienced, more productive agents can be linked with high LTV representatives. Agents trained in handling lower value representatives can offer appropriate products and services, thus optimally allocating customer service resources.

- During periods of extremely high incoming call activity, a representative's account number is linked to her lifetime value. Representatives with higher LTVs are given priority over those with lower LTVs.

- Lifetime value is also used in outbound calling efforts. The company is testing a "win back" effort to reenlist representatives who have left the sales organization. Among all representatives who have left, it is expected that those with highest lifetime value would provide the best return on investment of outbound calling effort.

Table 1

District	Acct #	Name	LTV Segment	LTV - Est	Action (Manager Notes)
1010	5429678	EVELYN D.	H	12,620	Request Assistance in Recruitment of New Reps
1010	3778373	AMY B.	H	7,110	Special Recognition
1010	3619684	WENDY F.	M	3,814	Provide Incentives for Further Growth
1010	4842830	FAVIOLA G.	M	1,274	May Leave - try to Retain
1010	3748210	LUCY S.	M	1,064	
1010	3750729	ANNA M.	M	1,021	
1010	3746420	THERESA S.	L	638	
1010	3770115	GUSTAVO C.	L	(179)	Unproductive - release
4555	3646117	MIRELLA H.	H	8,579	Special Recognition
4555	3645192	MARIA C.	H	6,748	Enroll for Beauty Training
4555	6075819	ANN S.	M	1,570	
4555	3637652	SUSAN P.	L	663	
4555	3646513	MARY M.	L	495	
4555	3775676	LEE P.	L	492	
4555	4076058	FRAN W.	L	0	Unproductive - release

Applications: Lifetime Value for ROI Analysis of Marketing Strategies

To promote a new product launch, marketing wants to send free samples to new representatives. Given the following information, we can estimate ROI.

- Available new representative population: 118,911
- Cost per sample: $2.50

We project 1.50% incrementally as a result of this promotion.

Depending on business objectives, we could consider four alternatives (see Table 2 and Figure 4):

1. **Optimum Penetration:** Send the product to representatives expected to have an LTV of $1,000 or more. We can reach 94% of this target group by promoting the top 70% of scored representatives (savings of $89,000 over promotion to all representatives).

2. **Budget Constraint:** Only $150,000 is available for this promotion. This allows us to promote the top 50% of scored representatives, which will reach 82% of the target group with LTV > $1,000.

3. **Maximize Profit:** Promote the top 35% of staff, reaching 70% of target population.

4. **Break-Even Analysis:** The break-even point would occur if we promoted the top 85% of representatives, reaching 98% of the target group.

Figure 4

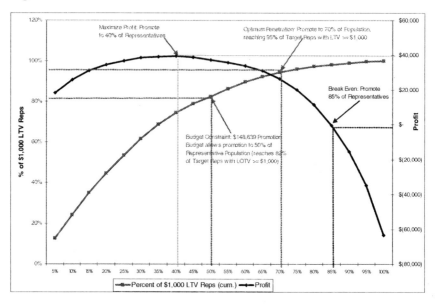

Table 2

Percent of Staff	Staff	Percent of $1,000 LTV Reps (cum.)	Avg. LTV	Avg. LTV (cum.)	Avg. Sales/Camp	Avg. Sales/Camp (cum.)	Incremental Sales (1.25%)	Cumulative Incremental Sales	Cumulative Promotion Costs	Profit	Note
5%	5,946	13%	$ 4,090	$ 4,090	$ 371	$ 371	$ 33,085	$ 33,085	$ 14,864	$ 18,221	
10%	11,891	24%	$ 2,713	$ 3,402	$ 254	$ 312	$ 22,608.93	$ 55,694	$ 29,728	$ 25,966	
15%	17,837	35%	$ 2,268	$ 3,024	$ 225	$ 283	$ 20,024	$ 75,717	$ 44,592	$ 31,125	
20%	23,782	45%	$ 1,974	$ 2,761	$ 206	$ 264	$ 18,331	$ 94,048	$ 59,456	$ 34,593	
25%	29,728	53%	$ 1,752	$ 2,559	$ 191	$ 249	$ 17,064	$ 111,112	$ 74,319	$ 36,793	
30%	35,673	62%	$ 1,568	$ 2,394	$ 185	$ 238	$ 16,487	$ 127,599	$ 89,183	$ 38,416	
35%	41,619	69%	$ 1,406	$ 2,253	$ 176	$ 230	$ 15,702	$ 143,301	$ 104,047	$ 39,254	
40%	47,564	74%	$ 1,264	$ 2,129	$ 168	$ 222	$ 14,974	$ 158,276	$ 118,911	$ 39,365	Maximize Profit
45%	53,510	79%	$ 1,141	$ 2,020	$ 159	$ 215	$ 14,180	$ 172,456	$ 133,775	$ 38,681	
50%	59,456	82%	$ 789	$ 1,897	$ 151	$ 208	$ 13,467	$ 185,922	$ 148,639	$ 37,284	Budget Constraint
55%	65,401	86%	$ 907	$ 1,807	$ 149	$ 203	$ 13,288	$ 199,211	$ 163,503	$ 35,708	
60%	71,347	90%	$ 773	$ 1,721	$ 145	$ 198	$ 12,908	$ 212,119	$ 178,367	$ 33,753	
65%	77,292	92%	$ 640	$ 1,637	$ 136	$ 193	$ 12,153	$ 224,272	$ 193,230	$ 31,042	Optimum Penetration
70%	83,238	94%	$ 512	$ 1,557	$ 117	$ 188	$ 10,469	$ 234,741	$ 206,094	$ 26,647	
75%	89,183	96%	$ 387	$ 1,479	$ 94	$ 182	$ 8,407	$ 243,148	$ 222,958	$ 20,190	
80%	95,129	97%	$ 266	$ 1,403	$ 68	$ 175	$ 6,052	$ 249,200	$ 237,822	$ 11,378	
85%	101,074	98%	$ 144	$ 1,329	$ 35	$ 166	$ 3,156	$ 252,356	$ 252,686	$ (330)	Break Even
90%	107,020	99%	$ 13	$ 1,256	$ (2)	$ 157	$ (222)	$ 252,134	$ 267,550	$ (15,416)	
95%	112,965	100%	$ (136)	$ 1,183	$ (51)	$ 146	$ (4,505)	$ 247,629	$ 282,414	$ (34,785)	
100%	118,911	100%	$ (395)	$ 1,104	$ (153)	$ 131	$ (13,639)	$ 233,990	$ 297,278	$ (63,287)	

Similar analyses utilizing the methods we have covered can be done for:

- Specific business segments: target beauty segment with high LTV (down to categories, brands, etc.)
- Selective field training programs/literature and support
- Incentives for sales meetings
- Recovery programs: Select high LTV representatives who purchased similar products

Through the combination of available data and data mining techniques, organizations can continue to enhance their operational efficiency.

Editor's Notes

The preceding chapter provided a clear picture on how data mining can help drive customer relationship management in an indirect way, through enhancing the efficiency of an existing sales force. Whether sales personnel are internal to an organization or external (as in this case) they play a vital role in achieving success for the firm since they are in direct contact with the consumer. As representatives of a company, a well-informed, trained and experienced sales person or sales team helps deliver the organizational message that the products and services provide for the customer. Data mining techniques applied to robust data sources enable strategic decision-makers, once again, to optimize organizational resources (sales force) to drive overall operational efficiency.

The next chapter extends the book's discussion of enhancing operational efficiency, this time in the healthcare industry. The material focuses on the utilization of overall business intelligence technology (of which data mining plays an integral role) in conjunction with the widely utilized strategic philosophy known as Six Sigma.

Chapter VI

The Healthcare Cost Dilemma:
What Health Insurance Companies Can Do To Mitigate Unsustainable Premium Increases

Russ Danstrom and Jeff Nicola
Anthem Blue Cross Blue Shield, USA

Introduction

The current state of the healthcare industry is one of flux and change. Countless articles and books have been written about the topic, and most suggest either putting control of healthcare into the hands of the consumer — much like we did with retirement planning — or government-based care rationing to a much greater degree than we already do today. So many factors have contributed to the rising costs of healthcare that one can barely grasp the grave realities of what the future holds. Projections of healthcare cost inflation have revealed future increases from 12% to 15% year-over-year into the foreseeable future. While quite disturbing, is this really surprising? Is there any other industry where purchase criteria does not include price? Can you imagine going to the grocery store, filling your cart, taking your groceries home and then getting the bill a few weeks later? Would you shop differently if you did not know the price? Who would buy the generic store brand, the larger size package, or wait for a sale? Nothing would ever go on sale. It would be difficult to make value decisions when benefits are known but not the price.

We are not arguing that healthcare purchasing is synonymous to grocery shopping, but rather, embarrassingly analogous — laundry detergent technology will not save someone's life. There are many drivers in healthcare that can be used to control costs, technological innovation being one of them, but the landscape is extremely complex and interdependencies among several "competing" constituents make coordination nearly impossible. While little can be done to control costs resulting from new technology, access to care, the aging population, or cost shifting from the government to the private sector, insurance carriers can focus on the following: provider quality standards, delivering benefit plans that force consumers to understand the costs and quality of healthcare procedures, partnering with other organizations to raise the awareness that lifestyle choices (smoking, eating, exercise) lead to the majority of healthcare costs, pushing for generic over branded pharmaceuticals, becoming more efficient and effective by optimizing their internal processes, and so forth.

This chapter focuses on managing the internal costs of doing business and generating incremental sales in a health insurance company, and covers a wide range of best practices, including why we must:

1. Measure "cost per sale" and "lifetime value derived from a customer" in the consumer market.
2. Leverage business intelligence tools to increase efficiency and effectiveness.
3. Use Six Sigma/change management techniques to help both identify   opportunities for improvement and to institutionalize change so that   insurers (and others) can be more efficient in delivering exceptional value to their customers at reasonable prices.

The bottom line is that most successful companies constantly strive to improve the coordination of strong leadership and data-driven decision-making, along with a relentless quest to optimize resources.

The Healthcare Insurance Organization

The healthcare insurance landscape in itself is very complicated and for some people, difficult to understand. So, prior to explaining what these organizations can do to control costs, we attempt to minimize the complexity by delivering a comprehensive, yet simplistic, view of the healthcare world. At a minimum, health insurance carriers offer healthcare products available directly to employers (B2B), and others that are available directly to consumers (B2C).

In the B2B market, there are two main types of affiliations an employer might pursue with an insurance carrier: either a fully insured (FI) or self-funded (SF) arrangement. In basic terms, an FI arrangement means that an insurance carrier administers and pays all contractual benefits for a given employer, whereas, in an SF relationship, they merely administer benefits for a given employer and the employer maintains the risk.

In order for companies to be successful in the healthcare insurance industry, careful planning, target marketing, and sales savvy are necessities. However, traditionally, the B2B market has tended to lean more heavily on the art of the sale (relationship selling) than the science of it. While this is also true for B2C business, direct marketers started changing this process in the early 1990s. It is far more difficult to build a book of business in the B2C market than the B2B world. Instead of landing an agreement with a 2,000-person company, B2C acquisition requires insurers to sell policies one at a time. And, it takes many policies to be able to sufficiently and profitably spread the risk. Since about 6% of the under 65 population in the United States buys health insurance for themselves, this can be like targeting a needle in a haystack. It can be very expensive to acquire these customers.

In order to efficiently and effectively sell B2C products, it is critical that a company knows that they are targeting the right people at the right time with the right message and at the right cost. Then they must determine how they can and should go about tapping the target market(s) both in terms of advertising (media and message) and sales technique (how easy are you to do business with?). At a minimum, we know that we must attack the B2C market using rigorous analytical techniques and data-driven decision-making, for any errors in sales and marketing strategy are extremely costly.

The Financial Data-Driven Approach
to B2C Acquisition

In today's economy, especially in the face of recent accounting scandals, companies and departments can ill-afford to employ laissez-faire financial planning or analysis tools. Rather, it has become paramount for corporate America to utilize logic and data to not only make decisions, but also to support actions. For every department in every company should constantly evaluate and be able to justify how it spends its money.

The B2C market not only requires careful planning and coordination between customer acquisition and finance departments, but also commands strong analytical knowledge of the segments that should be targeted. Finance is important in order for us to ensure that we are not overspending when we attempt to turn prospects into customers. Analytical knowledge of desired target segments, advertising campaigns and distribution channels is important so we know exactly where to spend the dollars that Finance has approved for us!

The need for data in the B2C market is critical and sensitive; it requires a company to have a solid data infrastructure in place, one that is easily accessible, logically built, relational in design, and reflects all the salient aspects of the current business strategy of the company. These needs require database architects to not only understand the technical aspects of building the database, but also to be in touch with the current business model of the company.

Once a solid infrastructure is built, businesses need users that can extract and then understand the data, working with it until they can turn data into actionable business information. Some of the basic data elements needed for analysis are: persistency (how long any given customer is retained by a company), benefit expense ratio (total claims dollars paid out by the company versus how much premium is taken in by the company), ongoing administrative costs, the companies' cost of capital, and customer acquisition costs (what it costs us in terms of advertising, sales and other costs of bringing prospects into the company). By possessing these data elements, one can begin to develop what is known as a Lifetime Value Model (LTV).

A properly calibrated LTV helps project how much money will be made or lost over a customer's lifetime (or lifecycle) with a company. It helps staff and management determine how much money can be spent to acquire customers (allowable acquisition cost), assuming a variety of profit margins, and accounting for (most of) the costs incurred by the customer during his or her affiliation with the company. All future cash flow streams are discounted back to today's dollars, thus providing us with a tool by which we can easily explain our expenses and projected return for any given customer acquisition activity.

Cost per sale is a basic yet often overlooked piece of the customer acquisition and LTV puzzle. If a company spends $100,000 on five different direct marketing campaigns and has no way to track which leads (or sales) came from which campaigns, how would that company ever know which campaigns to run next time? How can your direct marketing managers articulate how large their budget needs to be next year if they cannot tell you how much they spent this year to acquire customers through various advertising media? What if you were asked to cut 20% of your advertising budget? Would you be certain that you were cutting the 20% that produced the smallest amount of sales? If you measure your cost per sale, you know which programs yield the least sales...and hence, the highest cost per sale. Many marketers measure the number of sales and some even measure the cost to generate a lead. But without cost per sale value, these marketers assume that all leads convert to sales equally…quite a risky assumption. Building solid cost per sale models requires persistence and good data. Many arguments will ensue to determine the cost allocations. Tracking leads through to sales requires good processes and databases. Once you put the allocated costs and sales together, your decision-making and campaign prioritization will become much easier. It will also be easier to convince Finance that you *can* spend "their" money efficiently. However, once these basic elements are in place, marketers must continue to hone their campaigns and identify increasingly specific segments of the population to target. Business intelligence helps them do just that — doing more with the same or doing better with less.

Business Intelligence & A Healthcare Target Marketing Application

BI is a catchall acronym for an activity that really entails compiling, reading, manipulating, and crunching numbers — all of which has been referred to by writers as business intelligence. Some definitions include purely analytical applications — from OLAP (online analytical processing) to neural network technology (NNT) — but others include database development as well. Solid BI analysis can provide a competitive advantage for any company, for it has the power to increase effectiveness in decision-making and efficiencies in process execution. Some healthcare companies have used BI tools to: predict epidemics, streamline website design, forecast future claims costs, estimate sales, identify target markets, monitor process performance, and so forth. However, the key to reaping the benefits of BI applications resides in having the right people performing the analysis; they need to incorporate at least three elements:

1.   Understanding of the limitations of the data
2.   A strong facility in statistical techniques and modeling assumptions, and most importantly
3.   Intimate knowledge of the current business model

The most basic form of BI is spreadsheet manipulation of data, with perhaps some use of basic statistics. Yet, with the advent of OLAP, business users were given a tool with capabilities that might be explained by some as "a pivot table on steroids!" With OLAP tools, a user has the ability to look at variables using a variety of filters in an object-oriented environment (drag and drop). In other words, analysts were given the ability to take a multidimensional view of the dependent variables, which drive critical independent variables, such as "how many sales did we get in month 'x' and who were the people that bought our products?"

Though many varied skills are necessary to engage in a successful BI project, the cornerstones of success lie in the availability of clean data and people who have the ability to find the "hidden" statistical patterns within the data. Strong analytical and statistical knowledge is a given for any BI initiative, but creativity is paramount as well. One must be able to determine how to deconstruct data elements into their most granular forms; one must also understand parsimony when building models — that a good model can be replicated without too many complicated terms and transformations. In other words, the simpler the model, the better. And, if it must be complicated, the analyst should be sure that he or she could explain it. Next, we provide a case study of what one of these initiatives might look like; names and data elements have been disguised so as to protect the intellectual property of the constituents and company that provided our example. As you read through this case study, keep in mind that this work saved Company XYZ nearly $500,000 in only one year!

BI Case Study on the Couch-Potato Segment

Purpose

Previous research has shown that Company XYZ's couch-potato segment is one of their most profitable groups. As such, one of their goals was to increase the number of applications received from this segment. Over the past three years, Company XYZ had targeted this segment through direct mail campaigns based on purchased lists of couch-potato people. Their goal was to see what data could be appended to a mailing list that would allow modeling to: (a) increase their response rates, and (b) provide information that would allow them to better target this segment from a message/creative perspective.

This case provides an overview of the:

1. type(s) of overlay data that significantly increased the number of applications received from the couch-potato segment,
2. techniques used in determining those variable types, and
3. potential impact on the number of applications received if we had used this information in generating a mailing list.

Summary

Thirty-two columns of overlay data were purchased from Marvelous Warranty Card Company in 4Q 2000. Transformation

Table 1: Sample and Univariate Information

VARIABLE	VARIABLE PRESENCE (TIMES VAR = 1)	% OF SAMPLE	# APPS RECEIVED	PRESENCE OF VARIABLE WHEN APP RECEIVED?	RESPONSE RATE (APPS RECVD / VAR PRESENCE)	% INCREASE IN RESPONSE RATE
TOTAL SAMPLE	46,933	100.00%	922		1.96%	
When Pet's Age & Gender Info was present	29,128	62.06%	838	90.89%	2.88%	46.45%

of this data yielded 80 more columns of information for each customer record. Data mining tests demonstrated that there were eight variables that had an impact on the application receipt rate of the couch-potato segment. However, after further investigation we determined that "Pet's Age and Gender" variable had the biggest impact on application-received rates. The increase in response was 46% greater than the status quo (2.88% vs. 1.96%). See Table 1 for results.

Recommendation

Since results showed that using 62% of the mail file would allow us to have captured 91% of the applications received, Company XYZ ought to purchase "Pet's Age and Gender" overlay data from their list vendors from this point forward, and mail to the records which have populated values in this field.[1] In addition, ongoing verification studies should also be completed (e.g., set aside a control group for monitoring purposes).

Procedures

A total of 46,933 customer records were extracted for analysis. After creating new columns based on the demographic data we already owned and those purchased from a vendor, Company XYZ produced a total of 122 columns of data for each customer record. Several data mining experiments were conducted using a variety of regression, clustering, and decision-tree applications. This study included three analysis phases detailed as follows:

- *Phase 1 – Confirm Hypothesis that Presence of First Name Increased Response Rate:* The first phase of our research solidified previous research, which suggested that when we have the presence of telephone numbers, the applications-received rate was higher. Analysis confirmed that the presence of "First Name" data was the highest predictor of applications received.

- *Phase 2 – Test Only the Overlay Data and Specific Address Information:* In Phase 2 of the analysis, all information derived from Company XYZ's marketing database was removed (except PO Box and Rural Route presence), including phone number fields. By doing so they were able to take a finer look at which of the overlay variables impacted the application receipt rate. Similar data mining applications to those in Phase 1 were run in this phase.

Results of the analysis identified eight variables as having a strong impact upon the application receipt rate. The variable names, explanations of them, and general comments for each are stated as follows:

1. The presence of a value in the Pet's Age and Gender field.[2]
2. An answer of "Yes" to the presence of a Pet Age Range 0-3 years. This category is a subset of "Pet's Age and Gender", and as such, has an extremely high correlation with that variable. Therefore, we cannot use both variables for predictive purposes.

3. An answer of "Yes" to Home Ownership. This field reflects the likelihood of a consumer owning a home, and is determined from tax assessor and deed information.

4. An answer of "Yes" to Probably a Homeowner. For records in which home ownership is not matched, a value is calculated using Length of Residence, Dwelling Type, and other geodemographic characteristics. This value is calculated by a vendor's proprietary statistical model that predicts the probability of home ownership, ranging in confidence levels from 80% to 99%.

5. An Income Range greater than or equal to 400 but less than 500. This means that current census information identified a household as having an income 300% to 400% above the median Alaskan state level.

6. Length of Residence between .50 and 1.9 years. This field was extracted from vendor data, and represents time at current address. White page information as well as a USPS national address change file were used to determine this value.

7. An answer of "Yes" to the question of whether or not a "Multi-Company Direct Mail Responder" was a resident at the household level. In this variable, if one person in the household is a multi-company direct mail responder at the individual level, all other members of the living unit would be categorized as direct mail responders at the household level.

8. An address that contained a PO Box prefix.

- *Phase 3 – Evaluate Correlations & Incidence Rates of Variables to Reduce Number of Predictors:* After removing the variables that were highly correlated with one another, that is, those that explained the same variation in the data set, we were able to reduce the pool of predictive factors to seven fields. Furthermore, by examining the incidence of each of the variables, we were able to remove six more data fields. The most important test in this phase is to determine which of the overlay data fields we should purchase in the future. In order to answer this question, we needed to generate a file of only those instances in which "Applications Received" equals 1. In this data set, there were 922 applications received out of 46,933 records, which yielded a response rate of just under 2% (see Table 1).

Of the instances in which an application was received, in 838 times the "Pet's Age and Gender" field was populated with a value. That leaves us with 84 cases in which applications were received, but "Pet's Age and Gender" values were zero. Of those 84 cases that are unexplained by the "Pet's Age and Gender" field, we tested to see if any other variables would have led us to believe that there was in fact an application that was received. The results of this test demonstrated that there were only two cases where another variable (Income Index >=300 and <400) would have explained more of the variation in the data set.

Since we determined that there are no instances in which variables add incremental value to the results we obtained using the "Pet's Age and Gender" presence data, there is no reason to look further. The "Pet's Age and Gender" variable provides us with a 47% lift over the status quo application-received rate, and would have allowed us to reduce our mailing file by over 17,800 names — a 38% reduction in the mailing file! In other words, using 62% of the file, we would have captured 91% of the applications received.

As you can see, this case study provides an excellent example of an analytical study that points us in the direction of how companies might optimize resources, which ultimately could pass on savings to the healthcare consumer. However, the only way to accomplish this task is to alter business processes and change human behaviors — issues that plague companies that have not adopted methods to address them.

Six Sigma & Change Management

The combination of Six Sigma and change management is the third element (of many) that provides companies the opportunity to help control healthcare costs, at least from an administrative perspective. The central tenet of Six Sigma is to execute processes better, faster, and cheaper by minimizing defects, errors and complaints (all of which increase costs). Change management skill is what helps companies translate Six Sigma analytical findings into institutionalized business policies and procedures.

Six Sigma is a data-driven, process-oriented approach to problem solving, articulated directly with improving customer satisfaction. It is a philosophy and a mindset; it requires buy-in from the top down and the bottom up, and coordination everywhere in between. It requires its change agents to follow every detail of a given process throughout the organization. In the end, even though Six Sigma rests upon extensive analytical application, it is not merely a quality initiative or analytical exercise, but rather a business strategy in its own right. Six Sigma relies first on science, then on the art of data translation; it disallows conjecture, opinion and anecdotal information to dictate business protocol. By focusing on the customer first, Six Sigma can articulate our internal processes with what the customer wants — which, if executed properly, will increase profits, customer retention and growth rates by simply making your company easier to do business with.

Six Sigma *is* about numbers and measures; it follows the old business adage, "if you can't measure it you can't manage it". Ask yourself two questions: (1) Is it possible your company has been measuring the wrong thing with the right technique? (2) Or, that your company has been evaluating the right thing with the exact wrong technique? Of course, companies do it all the time, typically as soon as they lose focus of their customers' needs and wants.

One of the best ways to maintain customer focus is to constantly be in touch with the actual customer — and who knows better than those employees that are in direct contact with customers in the front line of the organization? Six Sigma forces us to turn to those people who feel the customers' pain and who hear their complaints; for they are the ones who truly help the Six Sigma change agent identify defects that need to be eradicated from broken, outdated processes. Following the principles of Six Sigma, we simultaneously stay in touch with the customer and empower our front line employees by asking their expert opinion regarding the way we do business day to day. On a basal level, if a company's leadership can keep its focus on these two "foundational" tasks, it can transform a culture from a good to an outstanding performer over a relatively short period of time.

The Six Sigma methodology generally follows a five-step process called DMAIC (duh-may-ik): Define, Measure, Analyze, Improve, and Control. Yet, successful Six Sigma projects require the project manager to possess not only the analytical acumen required to execute projects (about 35% of their time), but also the interpersonal and presentation skills to win over any audience and effect positive change (about 65% of their time). For the latter, we suggest reading John Kotter's "Eight Stage Process of Creating Major Change."[3] Although a thorough discussion of the nuances of Kotter's approach to change management is beyond the scope of this chapter, his approach matches well with the Six Sigma methodology, albeit from a non-analytical perspective. By joining the two methodologies into a comprehensive program, the probabilities of moving a company from "good to great" significantly increase.

We have discussed identifying process defects and where true expert knowledge resides, but how do we put these two approaches together? Six Sigma is a value-driven, structured approach that constantly keeps us focused on being efficient and effective, optimizing our resources, and staying ahead of the competition by creating an environment of constant innovation and improvement. Six Sigma also provides us with a powerful return on investment tool because it forces the user to prioritize projects based on bottom line impact. By maintaining this focus, we can work toward reducing administrative costs, growing profitable business segments, and improving service levels.

Kotter's first step in his process of creating major change calls for us to "establish a sense of urgency", to "examine…market and competitive realities", and to identify "…major opportunities" for improving the way we do business. If a company does not continue to stay ahead of the competitive curve, it will soon falter and lose market share, which ultimately will cause a company to fail in the marketplace. In the Six Sigma world, an average performing company operates at about three sigma, and that company is usually content with being "good" or "good enough". However, even if your company is performing at four sigma, there are still plenty of opportunities to improve. Just imagine a company that has three equal processes of equal volume and importance that are measured — one process is performing at one sigma, then next at three, and the final one at five sigma — then your company is performing at three sigma, you have one strong process, one average process, and one process that might cause your entire business model to fall apart. Convincing leadership and staff members to change the ways that they have always done things, especially in a "good" company, can be a challenge.

Just as Six Sigma requires top-down and bottom-up buy-in, so does Kotter's model. Kotter's Stage 2 details the importance of creating "a guiding coalition" that will lead and work as a team to make change happen. An engaged executive staff is a key component to the success of any change effort — after all, employees do move a little faster when their "big bosses" tell them that it might be a good idea to do so.

Furthermore, Stage 3 in Kotter's process calls for the development of a vision and detailed strategy for execution, which keeps the change effort on track. Within Six Sigma, Stage 3 applies to both deployment of a Six Sigma effort as well as project-specific work. The former would require a chapter unto itself. Regarding the latter, one can argue that the best ideas with poor execution plans are doomed to fail. Six Sigma requires project leaders to follow "roadmaps" that minimize the potential for projects to get off track. The structure of the Six Sigma mindset demands that the right expert team is identified and coordinated in a "just in time" environment, for there is no waste that is tolerable within the methodology.

Kotter's Stage 4 explains how important it is to communicate the change vision by any means available, and as often as possible.

Successful Six Sigma work requires a project manager to have no shame, to speak to anyone that will listen, and to exhaust all analytical and communication avenues up, down, and across stream. For it happens all too often that, due to lack of strong, clear, and persistent communication skills, solid analytical work never translates into actionable business information.

Kotter's Stage 5 discusses "empowering broad-based action", which includes: the "removal of obstacles, changing systems or structures that undermine the change vision, encouraging risk taking and nontraditional ideas, activities, and actions." Again, what good is it for a Six Sigma project leader to have the right ideas for changing a process, possess the data and logical argument to support the changes, but no power to implement the changes? We have stressed how important it is to have executive and frontline buy-in; however, it is also important to have strong buy-in from the middle. True power to change business processes, protocol, and behaviors resides within middle management (some proponents of Six Sigma might identify these people as being "Process Owners"). In sum, all levels of an organization must be "on board" with any change effort in order for it to be successful in the end.

Stages 6 and 7 in Kotter's paradigm, generating short-term wins and consolidating gains and producing more change, are well articulated with the Improve Stage in Six Sigma. What better way is there to sustain positive momentum than to deconstruct a process into its elemental form, address issues at a detailed level, and to constantly communicate and celebrate when each of the small problems are fixed? Furthermore, the Six Sigma change agent can capitalize on these wins by increasing her level of credibility, which ultimately will create opportunities for additional change action.

The Control Phase in Six Sigma is nearly perfectly aligned with Kotter's eighth and final stage, in which he discusses "anchoring new approaches in the culture". The final phase in the Six Sigma process differentiates the approach from all other process improvement initiatives. In order for a project manager to end a given project, a minimum of three months' audit data must confirm that the proposed solutions/changes did in fact make the overall process better. In addition, controls must be put in place in order to monitor the new process going forward.

There are four basic elements to any significant change effort that employs the Six Sigma methodology: talking, training, technology, and testing. Typically, one or more of these components are not aligned with the others very well, which causes processes to break down. Talking (communication) between and within departments is often a place in which processes suffer. Training often cannot keep pace with technological changes. And finally, if we do not constantly push the envelope and test new methods for accomplishing our goals, how will we ever get better at what we do?

Conclusion & Discussion

We began writing this chapter focused solely on demonstrating the utility of an analytical application (case study) within the healthcare industry; however, analysis is only the tip of the proverbial iceberg with respect to changing the way we do business and helping to control healthcare costs. Think of all the solid analytical work in your office that is buried within file cabinets or has found its way to the circular file — where no action was taken due to lack of empowerment, lack of communication skill, lack of being able to articulate bottom line impact of (not) engaging the project, and so forth. Business intelligence applications are part of change efforts, but much more structure, such as the approaches put forth by Six Sigma and Kotter, allows companies to execute and optimize resources.

Because demand for quality, affordable healthcare will only continue to grow as technological advances and the aging baby boomers come together over the next few years, the ability to control healthcare premium increases becomes that much more critical. Since about 82-85 cents out of every dollar of health insurance premiums goes to pay claims and an additional 10-13 cents covers administrative costs, there is little room for error in decision-making and in operational execution, in order to earn a profit.

National healthcare expenditures are currently around 14% to 15% of GDP and rapidly heading "north". Personal incomes are growing at 3% to 4% per year, while healthcare costs are increasing by approximately three times that level (10% to 12% per year), which makes our current healthcare model unsustainable in the medium and long-term. As such, healthcare will consume a bigger portion of personal incomes into the foreseeable future. With around two-thirds of the 41 million uninsured in the United States already unable to afford health insurance, it is likely that the uninsured population will grow. However, some factors could help contain the increases or possibly even shrink the uninsured ranks.

An improving economy that reduces the unemployment rate will provide more people with employer-based health insurance, possibly reducing the number of uninsured. But we still must find ways to mitigate the increasing cost of health insurance. National and regional measures may be taken to contain healthcare costs overall, and company-specific process improvement initiatives can also contribute to making healthcare more affordable by lowering administrative costs.

In this chapter, we discussed how we have worked to contain customer acquisition costs, which represent 25% to 45% of our administrative costs (with customer retention/service costs comprising the remainder). We argue that knowing your cost to acquire business and determining how much you can afford to spend force better decisions around customer acquisition (the same should be done with customer retention/service costs). This and other business intelligence, such as data mining and classical statistics, provides the information to guide solid fact-based decision-making. Coupling BI with the rigors of Six Sigma and change management allows health insurers the opportunity to streamline processes and take costs out of the business, which will help mitigate healthcare premium inflation and make quality healthcare more affordable for more people.

Endnotes

[1]   Matches in this case included "unknown" data because in this variable, "unknowns" indicated families that have pets, but those in which the gender of those pets is unknown. We are most interested in the presence of a value in this variable, as opposed to specific values within the coding itself.

[2]   This field is NOT to be confused with an answer of "Yes" in the Presence of Pets field, which only appears in our data set 7757 times. However, this field appears exactly the same number of times as when we have a match in the "Presence of Pets" field (which can be "Yes" or "Unknown"). This is a great double-check on the integrity of the overlay data purchase.

[3]   Adapted from John Kotter, "Why Transformation Efforts Fail," Harvard Business Review (March-April 1995):61.

Editor's Notes

The preceding chapter highlighted the ways in which data mining, overall business intelligence and the addition of Six Sigma applications can help healthcare insurance providers operate more efficiently. More specifically, these methods enable providers to better understand their consumers, along with successful or unsuccessful policies implemented to service them. By becoming more operationally efficient with its internal operations, this organization is able to better manage pricing policies, which in this case is to help reduce increases in premiums.

The following chapter also addresses the healthcare industry, but the focus is turned towards the utilization of data mining to help increase the efficiency of diagnosing illness, which can potentially lead to preventive treatment for a different type of customer, "patients".

Chapter VII

The Application of Data Mining Techniques in Health Plan Population Management:
Disease Management Approach

Theodore L. Perry, PhD, Travis Tucker,
Laurel R. Hudson, William Gandy,
Amy L. Neftzger and Guy B. Hamar
American Healthways Corp., USA

Introduction

Healthcare has become a data-intensive business. Over the last 30 years, we have seen significant advancements in the areas of health information technology and health informatics as well as healthcare modeling and artificial intelligence techniques. Health informatics, which is the science of health information,[1] has made great progress during this period (American Medical Informatics

Association). Likewise, data mining, which has been generally defined as the application of technology and statistical/mathematical methods to uncover relationships and patterns between variables in data sets, has experienced noteworthy improvements in computer technology (e.g., hardware and software) in addition to applications and methodologies (e.g., statistical and biostatistical techniques such as neural networks, regression analysis, and classification/segmentation methods) (Kudyba & Hoptroff, 2001). Though health informatics is a relatively young science, the impact of this area on the health system and health information technology industry has already been seen, evidenced by improvements in healthcare delivery models, information systems, and assessment/diagnostic tools.

Data mining techniques in the healthcare industry have evolved from the assimilation of artificial intelligence (AI) with large databases (Borok, 1997). Historically, the first AI techniques to become generally accepted in medical informatics were *expert systems*, developed in the late 1970s and early 1980s. Expert systems are algorithms designed to follow the same problem-solving steps that "real" experts might go through to derive a solution. For example, individuals recognized as being authorities in certain areas or domains (e.g., cardiology) are interviewed on their problem-solving methods. This information is programmed into a computer file called a rule base. Additionally, another file called a knowledge base is created containing the data needed to reveal the facts behind the rules. Usually prompted by a series of questions, an expert system is able to take answers from each question, search the rule and knowledge bases, and produce a result. Expert systems are currently in place to assist physicians with the identification of various medical events, such as myocardial infarction and stroke. These types of expert systems have become important tools because they are fast, unbiased, and, overall, more accurate than human experts.

Though expert systems are strong tools used extensively in the healthcare industry, they are not without their limitations. Limitations of expert systems in healthcare include (a) highly dynamic information on evidence-based medicine as well as treatment guidelines and (b) vastly different opinions from experts in a field where diagnosis is often times as much art as science. Faced with these shortcomings, AI began using data-driven approaches that attempted to learn from raw data, allowing for naturally occurring patterns and trends to define the rules that might govern them. Concurrently, advances in computer hardware and software during the 1980s and 1990s supported the development of new AI techniques based on a data-driven approach. An example of an AI technique that has gained popularity in recent years is neural networks.[2] Since neural networks are able to uncover patterns and trends in large data sets in which much of relationships between the variables are nonlinear in nature, they are well suited for healthcare informatics work. Neural networks are currently being used to predict patients who are at risk for future high medical cost and utilization (Perry, Tucker, & Hamar, 2001). These techniques are especially useful in identifying and targeting patients who are the best candidates for care management or disease management programs. An example of how neural networks have been used within a disease management setting is illustrated in the case study in this chapter.

Administrative data (e.g., healthcare claims information including medical, pharmacy, and laboratory data) are readily available from most health plans and managed care organizations. Though initially designed to facilitate claims processing activities at health plans, administrative claims data are very important in health informatics work, providing the first (and often the only) level of information for this type of research. Since claims data were not originally designed for healthcare or epidemiological research, there are obvious limitations to using these data. Consequently, there are numerous steps taken to transform and clean these data for research purposes. Nevertheless, since these data are often times the only source available, techniques have been developed to optimize the use of this information, which increase the probability of obtaining a data set exhibiting a higher degree of reliability and validity. Several of these techniques are discussed in further detail later in this chapter.

Perhaps the greatest issue facing our healthcare system today is the dramatic increase in patients suffering from chronic conditions such as heart disease, diabetes, asthma, and renal disease. Since it is estimated that there will be at least a 30% increase in the number of people with a chronic disease over the next 20 years, the healthcare industry has been pressed to seek delivery and technological solutions best suited to retard the ever-increasing gaps in healthcare treatment, delivery, and management. Disease management is an alternative available to assist our over-tasked healthcare system (Hunter & Fairfield, 1977). Disease management programs utilize methods for management, prevention, and health promotion activities that are based on medical best practices and evidence-based medicine. Success of disease management programs is usually evaluated on clinical/therapeutic improvement or compliance, cost reduction, and behavioral/emotional enrichment. Strong disease management programs depend on data mining techniques that maximize the ability to identify populations and, subsequently, target appropriate interventions to the right patients.

The purpose of this chapter is to discuss, from a disease management perspective, data mining techniques that have been commonly used in health plan population management. In order to describe the role of health informatics in this area, healthcare claims data, data preparation techniques and disease management data mining methods are discussed in further detail. Additionally, the development of claims-based identification and classification algorithms are discussed. Finally, a case study is presented that illustrates the application of data mining as well as artificial intelligence in disease management of a large commercial health plan population.

Healthcare Claims Data

When conducting healthcare research, there are many options for sources of data. The most common of these include data obtained from administrative claims, medical chart reviews, and interview surveys. In most cases, actual medical records would provide the most complete and detailed explanation of a patient's health and disease. However, reliance on medical records is very time consuming and costly. As a result, administrative claims data are an appealing and practical alternative in health research (Maclean, Fick, Hoffman, King, Lough, & Waller, 2002).

Administrative claims data can have many uses, such as:
- Identification of individuals with specific diagnoses to calculate prevalence within populations,
- Evaluation of the incidence of death and nonfatal complications during and after medical care,

- Comparisons of financial and utilization outcomes across payers, facilities, and specialties,
- Identification of providers and facilities with unusually high or low death rates, infection rates, or medical error rates, and
- Development of models to test hypotheses within the areas of clinical, financial, or utilization outcomes.

The most accurate results are obtained through a combination of claim types, such as the combination of medical claims and pharmacy claims (Quam, Ellis, Venus, Clouse, Taylor, & Leatherman, 1993).

Advantages of using claims data include relative low cost and availability, ease of trending over long periods of time, and control of reporting bias. Limitations of using claims data include typographical entry errors, missing information, inadequacy of the data to identify patient comorbidity, and lack of outcome information on functional status (Wennberg, Roos, Sola, Schori, & Jaffa, 1987). Nevertheless, when collected and used appropriately, administrative claims data can yield answers to a variety of health questions. Recently, research using claims data has become increasingly common and effective. Administrative developments such as the increased standardization of medical claims forms and electronic billing submissions have made healthcare claims data a more reliable and useful resource for health research.

Data Preparation Techniques

The role of data preparation in healthcare research cannot be overemphasized. For "intelligent" algorithms to effectively search data and detect meaningful patterns, the source data must be organized into a standard form. Data preparation begins during the extraction of data from the source systems. During this phase, data must be assessed (e.g., missing data, invalid data, and coding errors) and corrective adjustments made. Data cleaning and preparation is usually conducted prior to loading them into the study database, data warehouse, or respective data mart. Usually, this process is conducted using automated algorithms, though some data inconsistencies often require manual intervention.[3] Depending on the scope and purpose of the research effort, data can be converted (i.e., transformed) into either a binary format (e.g., 1s and 0s) or into some ordered variable format (e.g., 1, 2, 3).

Once data are in a standard form, a number of data transformations can be used to further enhance their value. Though there are numerous methods, two common transformations are data normalization and data smoothing. Normalization techniques include decimal scaling and standard deviation normalization. Decimal scaling preserves the original character of the data but moves the decimal point. Standard deviation normalization is typically employed with distance measures. While standard deviation techniques are effective, they radically alter the character of the original data, making interpretation slightly more complicated. Data smoothing is frequently used with regression techniques to reduce noise or random variation. Finally, when data cleaning and transformations are completed, these data are ready to load into the system (e.g., relational database, data warehouse, or data marts) (Weiss & Indurkya, 1998). Figure 1 illustrates a general IT approach to system architecture used to support health research based on claims data from health plans.

Figure 1: General Healthcare Claims Research Systems Architecture

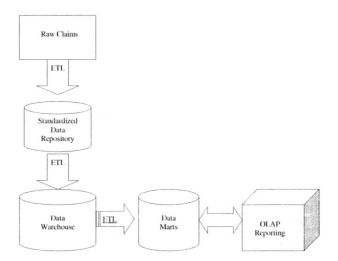

Development of Identification and Classification Algorithms

When attempting to accurately identify and classify data elements from healthcare claims for research and analysis, there are a number of issues to consider. Since no model is perfect, the key to finding the best model is to study the problem and determine the best approach for each situation. When building the algorithm, it may be beneficial to utilize such factors as inpatient claims, outpatient claims, laboratory results, or other data sources. The type of data used depends upon the purpose of the algorithm and the nature of the target variable (i.e., the variable of interest). For example, if the target variable is total healthcare cost, then it would be logical to include both inpatient and outpatient claims, as well as any other relevant monetary patient information.

During any classification problem, the goal is to properly assign individuals into the correct category or group. For example, if our goal is to iden   ᵓyone in the data set who might have diabetes, then our task is to accurately classify each individual as either belonging to the diabetes group or the non-diabetes group. However, unless our model is 100% accurate, there will be always be a few individuals who do not have diabetes and are mistakenly classified into the diabetes group (i.e., false positives), as well as some individuals who do have diabetes and are mistakenly classified into the non-diabetes group (i.e., false negatives). As illustrated in Figure 2, these types of classification problems can produce true positives, false positives, true negatives, and false negatives. An understanding of the relationship between all four of these groups is essential to resource allocation considerations as well as the reliability and validity of a study.

Healthcare claims are a major source of data used in building an identification model for use in a disease management environment. These claims can include inpatient, outpatient, professional,

Figure 2: Resource Allocation Matrix

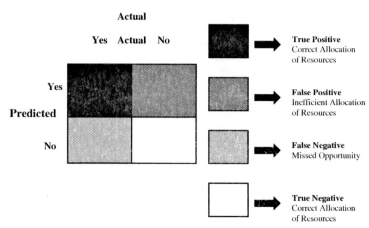

pharmacy, and laboratory services. These claims generally contain various procedure and diagnostic code fields that document the diagnoses and procedures that are part of a member's health services record. Other data that can be used in identification models include laboratory test values, demographic data, and data collected directly from members through survey methods. In the end, the types of data used depend upon the purpose of the model, the nature of the variable of interest (i.e., the target variable), and the data available during the construction of the model. As an example, if the purpose of the algorithm is to identify patients with diabetes, then it would be logical to include all relevant claims that identify a diagnosis of diabetes, procedures associated with the treatment of diabetes, medications prescribed for the treatment of diabetes, and laboratory tests that are diabetes-specific.

The concepts of sensitivity and specificity are very important in this type of classification problem. Sensitivity is the probability of obtaining a true positive classification; specificity is the probability of obtaining a true negative classification. Sensitivity and specificity are related in such a way that as one increases the other decreases (i.e., they are inversely related). When building a model, it is important to focus on the goal and purpose of the research effort and decide which is of greater importance — sensitivity or specificity. For example, an underlying algorithm can be adjusted to make it more sensitive to capturing true positives, or it can be adjusted to ensure that it captures more true negatives. However, adjustments in either direction will naturally increase the number of false classifications, unless it is a perfect algorithm, which is highly unusual.

Optimizing the model involves making choices that, in effect, establish cutoff points and define the sensitivity and specificity of the model (as well as the true and false positive rates). The final choice on how to group individuals generally takes into consideration the purpose of using a model, what is desired as an end result, and the potential consequences that can result from the correct classification and misclassification. In a disease management context, enough sensitivity to adequately identify the majority of disease members is needed, while not overburdening the management program with incorrectly identified members (false positives) that lead to an inefficient and wasteful use of the disease management program resources.

As an example, the sensitivity of a congestive heart failure (CHF) model would be the proportion of actual diseased members with CHF that the model classifies or identifies (from the review of available data) as having CHF. Alternatively, the specificity of the CHF model would be the proportion of actual non-diseased members with CHF that the model classifies (from the review of available data) as not having CHF. The false positives would be the non-diseased members that are incorrectly classified as having CHF. The false positive rate would be the proportion of the non-diseased members that have this incorrect CHF classification. The false negatives would be the diseased CHF members that are incorrectly classified as not having CHF. The false negative rate would be the proportion of the diseased CHF members that have been incorrectly classified as not having CHF. As in most of these identification problems, there is a trade-off in which increasing the sensitivity will also increase the number of false positives, or in which increasing the specificity will increase the number of false negatives.

Reliability refers to the consistency of a measurement, or the degree to which an instrument (or in our discussion, algorithm) performs the same way each time it is used under the same condition with the same subjects. In short, it is the repeatability of a measurement or identification. Validity refers to the accuracy of the measurement or identification being conducted. Using the example above, we would ask this question: Does a CHF identification model accurately and correctly identify members truly having the CHF condition? As with any statistical endeavor, reliability and validity are imperative. If the data, instruments, or the algorithm itself are lacking in consistency (i.e., they are not reliable), then, in all likelihood, we are measuring nothing more than error or noise. Similarly, if these items are not valid (as related to their appropriate constructs), then we lack accuracy. Consequently, no model can be successful if the tools behind it are lacking in consistency (reliability) or measurement accuracy (validity).

Disease Management Data Mining

Technological progress in data acquisition and storage capacities has resulted in the growth of huge databases, and this is especially true with respect to healthcare (Hand, Mannila, & Padhraic, 2001). The disease management (DM) industry has recognized the need for data mining, with the primary focus on deriving primary information from raw administrative claims. This knowledge discovery process turns data into usable information, which improves the healthcare delivery system and is important to the success of any disease management program. Disease management data mining has many facets, including identifying diseases and conditions, determining what variables are useful for predictive modeling, and evaluating a program's clinical and financial success.

The DM industry utilizes data mining techniques to identify disease cohorts for program inclusion. Disease identification models are developed using clinical expertise to determine which members in a health plan's population have the disease (e.g., diabetes). Different disease identification algorithms could vary in their level of sophistication (i.e., a combination of diagnosis, procedure, and/or pharmacy codes), but all have a common goal: maximizing true positive capture. Once developed, these algorithms are applied to administrative claims to identify health plan members for disease management program inclusion.

Data mining plays a key role in the identification of variables that would be used for predictive modeling. There are several methods for creating variables from administrative claims. The most obvious method is the summation and grouping of costs associated with each member (e.g., pharmacy, inpatient, and outpatient cost). The next method, which is more clinically based, is logically grouping diagnosis, procedure, and pharmacy codes. Finally, trending variables can be created by calculating the change in cost from the first quarter to the last quarter of the year. All of these methods are crucial for the development of accurate predictive models that properly identify which members within a disease cohort will likely incur the highest cost and will benefit most from more intensive interventions.

After the disease members have been identified, the predictive model has been applied, and a sufficient amount of time has elapsed (e.g., six months), the disease management program needs to be evaluated. Data mining is the method used to evaluate program success (e.g., a decrease in cost and utilization and an increase in compliance to medical best practices) by identifying the costs, utilization, and pharmacy patterns associated with the program members. Likewise, data mining is also used to determine the effectiveness of the disease management company's interventions.

Disease management companies have been able to capitalize on data mining by identifying the correct members for program inclusion, using predictive modeling techniques for stratifying members, and developing sophisticated methods for program evaluation. To optimize disease management efforts, all of these components must be successfully implemented.

Artificial Intelligence: Neural Network Predictive Modeling Case Study

The following case study is presented in this chapter as a general example of how a commercial disease management company might use data mining techniques.

Problem Overview

This study is a retrospective cohort analysis on members of a large commercial health plan located in the southeastern United States. The data mining challenge was to create a predictive model that accurately identified health plan members that would incur cost in the top 15% of the population. Since it is known that this high risk group is almost five times more expensive than the overall health plan average and represents over 70% of the health plan's cost, it would be ideal for disease management services.

Method

Three years of professional, pharmacy, and institutional claims for continuously enrolled members (i.e., those members who did not have a break in their membership in the plan) in two of this health plan's products were provided for approximately 55,000 total members. Following customary modeling procedures, two years of claims data were used to develop and calibrate (i.e., fine-tune) the model. Split-sample validation was used to ensure the reliability (i.e., repeatability) as well as the validity of this predictive model. Fifty-nine variables were extracted from claims data. A variety of methods, including decision trees, logistic regression models, and principle component analysis, were used to select the number of variables used by the neural network model. Predictors (i.e., independent variables selected as a subset of all risk factors extracted) were selected based on their predicted probabilities using decision trees. Those variables with the highest predicted probabilities were selected for inclusion in the neural net predictive model. This neural network processed 14 of the 59 variables to produce the best predictive model. A third year of claims data were used to assess the accuracy of this model.

Results/Outcomes

Results of the model were evaluated using receiver operating characteristics (ROC) curves on a Year One to Year Two cross-validation (i.e., withheld) data set, as illustrated in Figure 3. The

Figure 3: Year One to Year Two Receiver Operating Characteristic (ROC) Curve

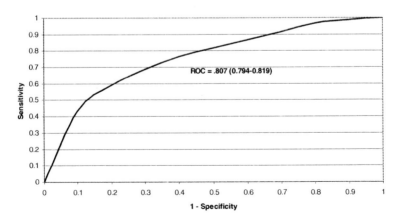

Figure 4: Year Two to Year Three Receiver Operating Characteristic (ROC) Curve

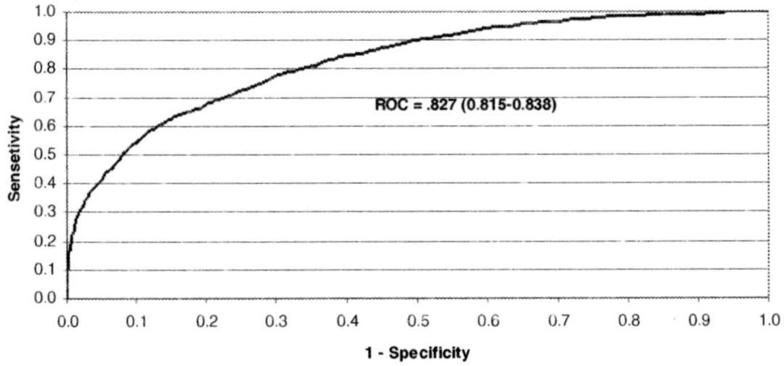

model showed a high level of accuracy on the Year Two cross-validation data set.

Additionally, actual Year Three results were compared to the results obtained from the predictive model to test the model's generalizability (see Figure 4). This high level of accuracy (83%) demonstrates the model's generalizability. Results from this model would be used to maximize resource allocation in a disease management setting. In other words, application of information derived from this model could be used to best manage resources, making sure the right efforts are being placed on the right patients at the right time.

Conclusion

"Often times, data must be tortured before it will confess the truth."

-Author unknown

"There are three kinds of lies: lies, damn lies, and statistics."

-Benjamin Disraeli

In this chapter we have described some data mining and artificial intelligence techniques that are currently being used in the disease management industry to optimize health plan population management. Since healthcare and healthcare delivery are changing at such a rapid pace, health informatics has become increasingly important in both the private and public sector. This area has become extremely data-intensive, with current data sources growing as well as new data sources appearing. The ability to manage and process large amounts of data has become essential in this industry. Fortunately, both computer hardware and software have evolved at a rapid pace, allowing researchers the opportunity to investigate behaviors, patterns, and trends that were technologically impracticable to examine only a few years ago.

Health informatics is a relatively new discipline, quickly gaining momentum as the healthcare and healthcare delivery industry becomes more and more reliant upon data management and data mining methods and techniques. In this quickly changing environment, companies must begin to investigate the use of these powerful tools in order to remain competitive. It is generally accepted that the healthcare industry is overburdened and under-resourced. To make matters worse, the number of people utilizing this system is growing at an extremely rapid pace, making it necessary for companies to explore creative options in order to attempt to meet this demand. Data mining methods will continue to develop to meet these challenges as researchers develop better techniques to transform data into information.

References

American Medical Informatics Association, The. 4951 St. Elmo Avenue, Suite 302, Bethesda, MD 20814. Available: www.amia.org.

Borok, L. (1997). Data mining: Sophisticated forms of managed care modeling through artificial intelligence. *J Health Care Finance, 23*(3), 20-36.

Hand, D., Mannila, H., & Padhraic, S. (2001). *Principles of Data Mining.* Cambridge, MA: The MIT Press.

Hunter, D.J. & Fairfield, G. (1977). Managed care: Disease management. *BMJ, 315,* 50-53.

Kudyba, S. & Hoptroff, R. (2001). *Data Mining and Business Intelligence.* Hershey, PA: Idea Group Publishing.

Maclean, J.R., Fick, D.M., Hoffman, W.K., King, C.T., Lough, E.R., & Waller, J.L. (2002). Comparison of two systems for clinical practice profiling in diabetic care: Medical records versus claims and administrative data. *American Journal of Manag. Care, 8*(2), 175-179.

Perry, T., Tucker, T., & Hamar, B. (2001). *Neural net predictive modeling at American Healthways.* White paper produced for American Healthways, Inc.

Quam, L., Ellis, L.B., Venus, P., Clouse, J., Taylor, C.G., & Leatherman, S. (1993). Using claims data for epidemiologic research. The concordance of claims-based criteria with the medical record and patient survey for identifying a hypertensive population. *Med Care, 31*(6), 498-507.

Weiss, S.M. & Indurkya, N. (1998). *Predictive Data Mining: A Practical Guide.* Morgan Kaufman Publishers.

Wennberg, J.E., Roos, N., Sola, L., Schori, A., & Jaffe, R. (1987). Use of claims data systems to evaluate health care outcomes. Mortality and reoperation following prostatectomy. *JAMA, 257*(7), 933-936.

Endnotes

[1]   Medical Informatics is defined by the American Medical Informatics Association *(www.amia.org)* as *...all aspects of understanding and promoting the effective organization, analysis, management, and use of information in health care. While the field of medical informatics shares the general scope of these interests with some other health care specialties and disciplines, medical informatics has developed its own areas of emphasis and approaches that have set it apart from other disciplines and specialties. For one, a common thread through medical informatics has been the emphasis on technology as an integral tool to help organize, analyze, manage, and use information. In addition, as professionals involved at the intersection of information and technology and health care, those in medical informatics have historically tended to be engaged in the research, development, and evaluation side of things, and in studying and teaching the theoretical and methodological underpinnings of data applications in health care. However, today medical informatics also counts among its profession many whose activities are focused on dimensions that include the administration and everyday collection and use of information in health care.*

2   Neural networks are modeled after the way a human brain works. As an alternative to traditional computer models (based on ones and zeros), a neural net uses processing elements (an electronic model of a neuron) to create connections between these elements. Over repeated iterations, the model learns the best weights and organization of these processing elements. The output of a neural network model is determined by the best fitting weights and element organization.

3   Most large database or data warehousing projects have adopted the ETL process (extract, transform, load) to ensure data quality and integrity. There are many commercial ETL software packages available.

Editor's Notes

This past section clearly illustrates the growing importance of an organizational and industry resource, and this is "data". As data resources become more robust, decision-makers can effectively utilize an assortment of innovative technologies, including data mining techniques and expert systems. By transforming data into information and ultimately a knowledge resource, healthcare providers can more effectively treat patients in situations in which the result is perhaps one of the most important operational outcomes we know...the reduction of illness and a healthier individual.

The next chapter will divert from the world of healthcare and address another essential industry sector, the world of advertising. This section will illustrate the power of data mining in better estimating the impacts of advertising activities on organizational performance.

Chapter VIII

Toiling in the Media Data Mines:
How Do You Know If the Ad Budget is Actually Working?

Robert Young
PHD Canada (subsidiary of Omnicom Group Inc.),
Canada

Introduction

At PHD Canada, we deal in *"time and space"* — a phrase used when the term *"media management"* draws blank stares at cocktail parties. There are thousands of people like us, in hundreds of companies like ours, responsible for managing advertising media budgets. We all go to great lengths to create crisp target group definitions for consumer brands. We determine which media channels should be employed in support of our clients' messages — time and space channels such as TV, radio, magazines, Internet, and newspapers. We recommend when our clients should run the media weight afforded by their budgets. And finally, we recommend how the weight should be distributed throughout the country, in which cities and which regions.

Media Is Where the Money Is

Major advertising budgets are distributed roughly 90/10 between the acquisition of media time and space (the 90) and creative development and production (the 10). And so, media expenditures are a big part of the total ad budget, and the total ad budget is, for most consumer marketers, a very significant cost item for the company as a whole. That is why the CFOs at the companies that own the brands we manage always ask the following question: "How do you know if the ad budget is actually working?" We think we have the answer. This chapter outlines how our company applies data mining techniques to mass media campaign history. We'll show you what we have done and what we have found.

Which Half is Wasted?

"Half of my advertising is wasted; I just don't know which half" is a quote from the 1920s or perhaps the 1930s (debate rages over source and date). The quote proves that concerns about return on advertising investment are as old as modern advertising itself.

The pressure on marketing departments to justify marketing and advertising investments has recently intensified. There is a new recognition that brands are valuable entities. Good brands hold equity. They have value beyond their ability to generate annual sales revenues and profits and so they can single-handedly build shareholder value. Marketing expenditures take on new importance because it is generally recognized that marketing effort is required to maintain brand value. Corporate officers understand the need for these expenditures but they desperately want assurance that the moneys are being spent effectively.

Some Media Communication Channels Are Easily Measured

"How do you know if the ad budget is actually working?" is readily answered when marketers use fully accountable communication channels. Direct response marketing, for example, is characterized by the instantaneous tracking of orders and leads. In turn, every order can be "fused" back to a specific commercial or ad. Each media dollar can be evaluated on a "cost-per-order" or "cost-per-lead" basis. Modern marketers have also embraced one-on-one consumer communication. Particularly heavy, brand loyal consumers are identified by name and address, held in a database and subjected to individualized messaging. These efforts can also be made fully accountable. The Internet is another channel that has the ability to track individual response to messages. These communication channels are characterized by response transparency.

But marketers still invest heavily in the more traditional mass media for several reasons. Mass media is cost efficient when broad target groups are involved. Turnaround times can be short. Dramatic results can sometimes be produced. Brand messaging can be fully controlled. It is a high profile option (and it also boosts clients' egos). The bad news? It is devilishly difficult to measure the responsiveness of mass media efforts. Unlike direct response and one-on-one marketing, there are no direct feedback loops. Even in clean test market situations it is difficult to isolate media's impact on brand sales because dozens of other marketing tactics are usually running simultaneously to the mass media activity. So when attempting to measure the impact of your ad budget, data mining is often the only way to go.

Data Mining is the Only Way to Go

Neural networks, desktop computing power and user-friendly stats software packages make data mining readily accessible to media people. There is finally a way for the media community to better understand the implication of their media planning and buying actions. The theory that advertising action has consumer reaction takes on distinct reality when data mining disciplines are applied to past campaigns. With this technology, we can better identify relationships between target variables (like sales) and driver variables (such as promotion and price), which ultimately enhances our ability to allocate resources in this industry.

Put Yourself in the Consumer's Shoes

Media planners, researchers and buyers tend not to have specialized stats training and so we rely heavily upon the stats packages built into data mining software tools. Sometimes, presentations of important consumer and brand insights to our advertiser clients turn into sizzling interrogations from Bayesian experts, instead of focusing on the valuable relationships that seem to exist between media activity and consumer actions. The media profession, though lacking in the science and theory of statistical modeling, more than overcompensates because of familiarity with the brand's consumer and hands-on experience with the communication dynamics of mass media.

If we mine with our feet firmly planted in the consumer's shoes, we usually strike gold. For example, a stats purist will want to isolate a full compliment of laundry detergent price variables such as the brand's price, the competitors' prices, the prices by unit and the prices by equivalent sized unit. The consumer-centric media

Figure 1

How To Calculate *Relative Price* Laundry Detergent Example (4 weeks ending June 19th 2003)		
	Total Category	Brand X
SALES	$21,498,917	$4,911,593
UNITS	3,116,583	666,648
SALES/UNIT	$6.90	$7.37
RELATIVE PRICE	100.0	**106.8**
One unit is a case containing product capable of delivering 125 washloads.		

person will immediately look at pricing the way a consumer looks at pricing — the brand's relative price (perhaps in the form of an index) per wash load. If a consumer is buying laundry detergent because of price, they will evaluate on the basis of cost-per-clothes-washed. The media specialist knows this because a good media specialist thinks like his or her consumer target.

To Each Brand Its Own

We have analyzed dozens of brands, hundreds of times with data mining. A handful of constant "truths" have emerged and we review many of these solid understandings in this chapter. But we have been surprised by the number of times variables that stand out as strong drivers for some brands, weaken considerably when evaluated for other brands. For example, we have conducted 22 separate econometric studies for a large, international packaged goods client, and the TV medium was found to be the most effective channel, in 16 of the 22 cases. The magazine medium was found to have been the most effective channel for five separate brands. Each brand has the capacity to appeal to consumer segments that can vary significantly in terms of their media preferences. In two cases, the demographic makeup of the TV-centric brand's target group appears to be identical to the magazine-centric brand's target. And so it must be concluded that some brands are able to communicate their benefits more effectively in one medium over another.

This finding plays havoc with media and marketing theorists who believe there are overall, macro theories of communication that can be evenly applied to all brands. Our findings suggest that every brand can find a way of becoming an exception one way or another. And in some cases, even the deepest understanding of a consumer target group and their media usage habits can produce channel plans that miss the mark. The lesson is this - build rules of thumb, brand-by-brand.

There are Two Parts to This Puzzle

The advertising impact puzzle is best examined by breaking down the ad process into two chronological parts. Part one is communication — the ad or commercial runs, the consumer is exposed, some degree of communication occurs. Focus groups, creative pre- and post-testing, and advertising or message recall awareness tracking are techniques used by advertisers to determine just how much communication has taken place between the brand message and the consumer.

Part two of the advertising process involves behavior. This is the more complex, but ultimately the more rewarding field of investigation — determining what kind of effect advertising has on the consumer's behavior in the grocery store, bank or car dealership — advertising's impact on sales levels.

Part One–Mining Inside the Communication Arena

Most major advertisers monitor consumer communication by "tracking" their advertising activity. A weekly sample of target group consumers is contacted and questions are asked. Brand awareness, advertising awareness, message awareness and various types of recall (top-of-mind or share-of-mind) scores are captured, each over consecutive weeks. Tracking has traditionally been conducted in "pre" and "post" waves of interviewing. The "pre" establishes awareness benchmarks before the ad campaign breaks and the "post" provides a glimpse into the extent of the consumer's growth in awareness as a result of the advertising activity. The research houses overseeing this process will often overlay the brand's communication scores against the brand's media activity. Sometimes norms are provided for the appropriate product category and commentary will be made about how the brand exceeded or performed below expectation. Kudos or blame will be laid at the doorstep of the creative or media.

Tracking is Best Done All the Time

Recently, marketers have begun to recognize the value of 52-week awareness tracking. There is, after all, immense value in understanding what happens to consumers when the brand's media activity is *not* running.

The analyses fueled by the 52-week tracking database usually produce lots of heat but little in the way of light. Was it the media or the creative that caused the good/bad results? What is the relationship between media weight and ad awareness? How much weight is enough? How much is too much? Consumer communication in the form of 52 weekly data points makes for great data mining. The target variable is one of the awareness or recall scores and there are usually several to select, one at a time. The driver variables take the form of weekly expressions of media weight (Gross Rating Points) or weekly expenditures for each medium utilized by the brand. Weight or expenditure levels generated by competitive brands can be easily obtained through monitoring services. In this way, relative weight for our brand can easily be calculated. The software package also gives us the ability to consider "binary" driver variables such as Yes and No, or words to characterize creative campaigns or the events being promoted.

We have been conducting data mining of awareness tracking data for several years for a quick service restaurant chain and a nationwide family dining chain.

Here is a summary of the learning.

1. *The competition has little impact on a brand's ability to get its message across.* Strong model and test scores were generated between the brand's media activity and the various

Figure 2

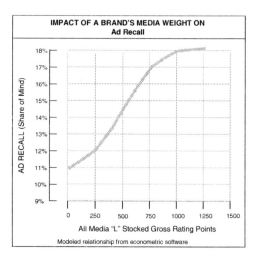

message recall scores from the tracking studies. Media activity being generated by the brand's competition did not seem to interfere with our brand's communication results. In other words, the consumer's ability to recall our brand's message tended to be a function of our media program and did not increase or decrease as a result of weight levels being produced by competitive brands (Figure 2).

2.   *Brand awareness is, however, affected by competitive activity.* Media campaigns support messages and in the case of these restaurant campaigns, the messages were specifically focused on meal events or promotions. We noted above that more weight produced more message recall. Brand awareness, on the other hand, resisted the effect of the brand's media weight. Rather, we found overall brand awareness was impacted by the brand's relative weight. Relative weight is determined by simply subtracting competitive media expenditure from our brand's media expenditure. The more positive (or less negative) our brand's relative media expenditure, the higher our brand awareness score became (Figure 3).

Figure 3

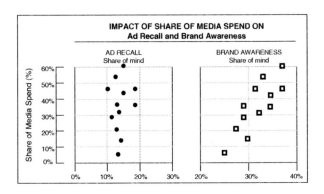

3. *Data mining helps identify competitive sets.* Brand managers spend a lot of time and energy defining competitive sets for their brands. Often the result is a kind of "wish list". The competitive set is comprised of brands the marketer would like "for company". Consumers, not marketers, should define competitive sets and data mining helps us understand the consumers' preferences. We found a relationship between our restaurant advertiser's brand awareness scores and the brand's media spend relative to the competition but we also found that the model and test fit scores moved up and down depending on the number of restaurants we added to the competitive list. In the end, the best list was the longest list. In other words, the consumer considered all restaurants to be competing for the pocketbook. It was a very good lesson for the brand manager, who thought the list should be more restricted.

4. *Messages echo differently between TV and radio.* Media people are familiar with the idea of message echo or lag. Media "Adstock" is the official word we use to describe a diminishing returns pattern that often occurs after the message has aired. Adstock occurs because of consumer memory. One simple Adstock pattern places full value on media expenditures in the week of commercial airing (100% in week 1), 80% of expenditure in week 2, 60% in week 3, and 20% in week 4. In all of our mining work, where we examine relationships between media weight and message communication, we run three alternate adstock patterns, one at a time — Nstock (no echo at all), Adstock (the pattern above) and Lstock (longer echo pattern). The results gave us the best TV message recall model and test fit scores when Lstocked TV expenditures were used. Radio recall, on the other hand, correlated best

Figure 4

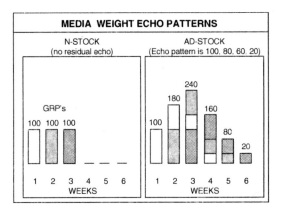

with Nstock patterns. This is an important media insight. The TV medium resonates over time while the radio medium packs all of its memory punch in a shorter time span (Figure 4).

5. *Promotion comprehension and participation are less reliant on media.* Our mining analysis can incorporate promotion, creative, and event variables by simply allowing for the inclusion of English language identifiers. When the data source is created, promotion names can be added to a column against the appropriate weeks. This becomes a particularly interesting analysis when multiple-year brand histories are examined and promotion names get repeated a few times. Promotion comprehension and participation scores from the ad tracking study are, as you would expect, particularly susceptible to promotion name. The consumer communication picture that emerges is like a plateau of comprehension, created by the promotion name, with additional peaks and valleys of comprehension on top of the plateau driven by weekly media support. We found the promotion comprehension levels were highest for repeat promotions and lowest for the promotions

Figure 5

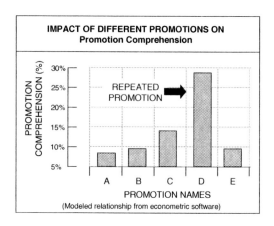

that were launched for the first time. Again, this might appear to be self-evident, but it clarified, once and for all, the value of recycling a short list of promotions through the year. Consumers respond to familiar messages, it seems (Figure 5).

6. *Brand awareness or promotional recall but not both.* Pity the poor advertiser struggling with the dual objectives of increasing overall brand awareness as well as building the consumer's understanding of a promotion or special event. Our data mining work has demonstrated that you cannot do both well with one media budget. Brand awareness builds when a brand's media expenditure increases relative to the competition, and this usually calls for a concentration of the media budget in periods of time when competitive noise levels are at their lowest. Front-end loading the brand's media expenditure during the promotion period, on the other hand, best maximizes a promotion's ad awareness and recall levels. That is because the TV medium's ability to generate echo or

residual awareness long after the commercial airs suggests that the TV expenditures should be scheduled early on in the promotional window, so the full echo benefit runs before the promotion expires. The media planner cannot schedule weight during a lull in competitive activity (to maximize brand awareness) and front-end load (to maximize message recall) simultaneously. In this case, the lessons from data mining help the media professional avoid a common pitfall — trying to do too much and succeeding at nothing.

7. *All media contribute.* Ad tracking research usually captures message recall scores for each of the media being utilized. Recall scores are captured by media because the messages can be different between media channels. For example, the TV message might focus on appetite appeal while the radio message focuses on the price point. When we treat a medium's recall score as a target variable, TV's for example, we make a point of examining all media expenditures (TV, radio, out-of-home) on the driver variables list. The key driver variable is inevitably the medium in question — TV expenditure is the key driver of TV recall — radio expenditure is the key driver of radio recall. But we usually find that all media impact, to varying degrees, the recall of each individual medium. For example, radio expenditures were found to have lifted TV recall scores. And TV in particular lifts the recall scores for all media. Data mining helps to quantify the degree of confusion experienced by the consumer when multiple media channels are supporting an ad campaign. The mining exercise helps us to quantify the credit being assigned, incorrectly, to a medium by confused consumers (Figure 6).

Figure 6

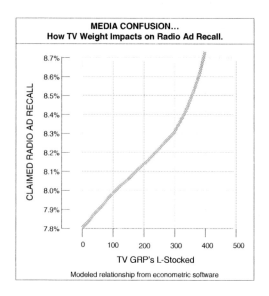

MEDIA CONFUSION...
How TV Weight Impacts on Radio Ad Recall.

CLAIMED RADIO AD RECALL

TV GRP's L-Stocked

Modeled relationship from econometric software

Part Two–Mining Consumer Behavior

A brand's business objective is enunciated early in the media planning process, and most of these contain the word "sales" and "sales share". As a result, the vast majority of data mining work that involves seeking and understanding consumer behavior will translate into understanding what driver variables drive sales.

Share Is the Way to Look at Things

We have found that sales share (market share) is a particularly helpful way to look at the sales variable. One advantage to incorporating this is that it neutralizes the influences of seasonality. Share numbers are driven by the nature of the competitive set that has been created and the share levels become larger as the competitive set shrinks. When we are conducting data mining exercises with brands, we will often construct a wide range of optional competitive sets, along with the resulting optional brand share history trends. Each optional set of data is mined and the model/test fit scores examined. Often the scores improve as the competitive set definitions move in a certain direction. For example, we examined a shampoo/conditioner brand in a series of competitive sets that contained premium priced brands. The model fits (e.g., explained variance of the model) improved as the competitive sets moved towards the most premium priced grouping. The consumer had spoken through the language of data mining — "I consider this brand to be part of this group and I become most predictable when you, the data miner, think of me in this way."

Most of the data mining work we have performed, when relating to sales modeling, has been for packaged goods brands in the food, home care and personal care fields. The following four lessons have accumulated over several years of working in this area.

1. *Percent share of voice is a bad way to look at the media variable.* Let's say my brand spends $100,000 in a week in advertising and the total competitive set spends $1 million. My brand's "share of voice" (SOV) is 10%. Share of voice is easily calculated, commonly used and immediately understood, but it makes for a lousy driver variable. Consider the example of another week of media activity — my brand is spending $300,000 and the competition is spending $3 million. The SOV is still 10% but the weight landscape has significantly changed. Or take the situation in which our brand is in weight hiatus (no weight) while the competition spends $1

million. Would we express our brand's SOV in this case as being 0%? If the competition increases its spend to $2 million, our SOV stays at 0%, but clearly the competitive forces have changed dramatically. We have found that share of voice percentages are simply inadequate numerical representations of a brand's relative media weight. SOV just is not sensitive enough.

2. *Relative, net media is a much better measure.* A far better metric for quantifying media "noise" in the brand marketplace, is net, relative media spend. This is calculated by quantifying the brand's spending level and subtracting from that figure the total spend generated by the competitive brands. The NRMS level will inevitably work out to be a negative number (unless the brand is extremely dominant). The brand will move to a $0 middle ground or equilibrium if there is no activity in the market place or if the brand spends an amount equal to the competition.

    Some have criticized this approach because all brands are effectively given an equal weighting. Why not keep the individual brand media spend levels operating as separate variables and let data mining models "make the call"? To our way of thinking, the merged media spend approach is the closest replication of how consumers think. Think the way the consumer thinks. Competitive brand spending produces a wall of noise, which hits the consumer. The ability to separate any one brand from the rest of the pack grows as the NRMS for any one brand increases. We have found that test and model scores improve dramatically once we treat the media variable in this way (Figure 7).

Figure 7

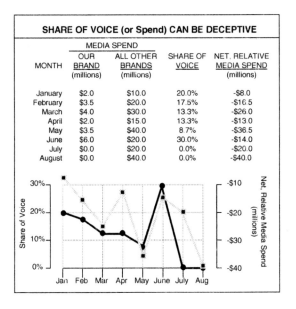

SHARE OF VOICE (or Spend) CAN BE DECEPTIVE

MONTH	OUR BRAND (millions)	ALL OTHER BRANDS (millions)	SHARE OF VOICE	NET, RELATIVE MEDIA SPEND (millions)
January	$2.0	$10.0	20.0%	-$8.0
February	$3.5	$20.0	17.5%	-$16.5
March	$4.0	$30.0	13.3%	-$26.0
April	$2.0	$15.0	13.3%	-$13.0
May	$3.5	$40.0	8.7%	-$36.5
June	$6.0	$20.0	30.0%	-$14.0
July	$0.0	$20.0	0.0%	-$20.0
August	$0.0	$40.0	0.0%	-$40.0

3. *Adstock is affected by consistency of creative message.*
    The echo or residual awareness generating power of media
    advertising was discussed in the Part One section of this
    chapter. We noted that the echo effect produced by media
    weight could be short/nonexistent (Nstock), of average dura-
    tion (Adstock) or longer than normal (Lstock). We observed
    that different media channels possess different durations of
    echo. In our example, TV possessed Lstock while radio's
    echo was best categorized as Nstock. We have found that
    brands also possess echo patterns. Never assume that one
    pattern of media weight or expenditure, calculated out over
    time, can be applied equally to all brands. Each brand needs
    to be analyzed as a variable against each of the three main
    patterns, one at a time.

As a result of performing a number of separate brand examinations we noticed a pattern. Brands that had been in the marketplace for several years (decades) that had enjoyed consistent levels of media support over several years and that had marketed themselves off one consistent creative platform over several years, inevitably possessed Lstock media residual patterns. Brand launches or brands with only a year or two of history under their belts exhibited Nstock media patterns. There just had not been enough time for these brands to generate equity. Brands that had been available in the marketplace for years but had recently experienced a new creative "relaunch" also possessed short Adstock patterns. These patterns of media weight or expenditure help to quantify the value to a brand of marketing consistency. Media weight, say 100 TV GRPs, aggregate up to almost 300 GRPs when calculated through an Lstock pattern. The Nstocked effect of 100 GRPs is just 100 GRPs. In other words, media investment, when applied to a brand that has been consistently supported, produces up to three times the return over an inconsistently supported brand. A brand that has received consistent treatment over the years requires less and less media weight and expenditure to maintain its position, sales share and communication recall scores.

4. *Innovation is the ultimate variable. But how can it be measured?* We have encountered criticism from modelers who note the absence of "innovation" as a driver variable in our brand sales data mining work. Innovation, in their estimation, is more than an important variable — it is the key characteristic driving a brand. In a new brand launch, the presence of innovation produces success. If innovation is

lacking, the brand will die. Few can or will argue with this point.

We have, in most cases, not included innovation as a driver variable in our data mining work, but it should also be noted that we have never used data mining as a tool for predicting launch success rates for new brands. Our work has focused on brands that exist in the marketplace. We look at three-year intervals of time (the basic data base provided by A.C. Nielsen is a rolling three year period, 13X4 week periods per year) and examine a brand's share movement in period one (with its existing level of perceived innovation) to that same brand (and perception of innovation) through to period 39 (13 periods times three years = 39 periods). Innovation remains constant through this process unless some significant re-engineering of the brand has occurred.

And so we believe we can avoid dealing with the innovation variable in "steady-state" cases — situations in which the brand has three years of share history following launch, assuming no significant modifications have been made to the brand during the examination period.

We did approach the issue of innovation in one instance in which the brand in question was from the ice cream product category. Brand management suspected sales improvements occurred for the brand when new flavors or treatments were issued. For example, a new "figs and walnut" flavor variation would carry the expectation of a mild share jump for the brand. The bigger and more dramatic the variation, the bigger the share jump. We quantified this variable by creating separate columns of data representing new flavor initiatives. Each new flavor got its own column. The word "Yes" was placed against the four-week period of launch and for two additional four-week periods thereafter. In this way a three, four-week period was identified as housing the impact of the new variant. The resulting analysis that obtained acceptable model and test scores placed small impact scores against each of the variants, but they added up to a significant "total innovation" effect and in the end, the brand manager could see that the new variants accounted for about 15% of the brand's share growth.

The Waste is Much Smaller Than Half

Those who believe half of the advertising effort is wasted clearly do not data mine their media history. If they did, they would be able to trace the lines and curves that describe the relationship between "all" of their media expenditures and their sales share movement. They would notice that all of the media money has a range of impact on brand growth, ranging from shallow/weak plot lines to steep/strong impacts. Obviously, some brands respond more favorably to the media variable than others. But in most cases, cutting out half of the brand's media expenditure simply reduces the share-raising ability of the media variable by one half.

The delayed impact characteristic of media also leads marketers to undervalue the power and influence of media expenditures. For Lstocked brands, media expenditures generate only about one half of their total positive brand impact in the month the media expenditure is actually incurred. Far too often, the full media investment is applied against only the brand's sales return in the first month. Benefits that accrue to the brand in the second, third and fourth months are not taken into consideration. Data mining, with properly Adstocked treatments of brand media expenditure patterns, ensures that full return is applied to the media investment.

Media and Sales. A Straight Line Relationship More Often Than Not

Most media and marketing theorists, as well as marketing consultancies, characterize the relationship between media weight or expenditure and communication or sales results in a nonlinear way. Some use flattened "S" shaped curves while others employ curves that grow quickly at first and then slow into diminishing returns. In all of our work, we found the best model and test fit scores produced straight line or almost straight line relationships between media and sales. Perhaps we have been looking too closely to the data set. In other words, it is possible we are dealing with a narrow range of media weight and expenditure levels. Perhaps if the historical data contained wider swings in media weight levels the curves would have emerged, but they did not, and this makes our lives easier. In our real, media practitioner, day-to-day world, we will be generally facing simple straight lines. The notions of diminishing returns and thresholds undoubtedly exist under some extreme conditions for our brand, but these are theoretical notions that need not disrupt 90% of our day-to-day planning work.

It's Like the Wind

Media support is like the wind. It is invisible and difficult to measure and track, but it can be harnessed, once understood. Data mining and econometrics are the tools whereby media people can better understand the impact of media investment on communication advancement and brand sales share. Understanding how media work empowers the media practitioner. When questions regarding return on media investment are answered, senior management becomes more confident and the likelihood that the brand will be supported consistently over time is greatly increased. That, in turn, improves the return on the media investment.

Editor's Notes

Advertising is the mechanism by which organizations across industry sectors communicate a message describing their products and services to the consumer market. Some initiatives are successful, while others are not. Data mining and econometric modeling techniques enable organizations to optimize their resource allocations in marketing their message through advertising, as they provide a quantifiable connection between resources expended and results attained. With the power of quantitative modeling, decision-makers can better allocate budgets to those mediums that achieve the most positive results.

The following chapter addresses another aspect of the advertising industry but focuses not on the "brick and mortar" environment but the "click and mortar", online spectrum. As e-commerce initiatives continue to expand in the evolving information economy, estimating the returns to online activities will no doubt grow in importance.

Chapter IX

Audience Measurement Applications for Online Advertising and E-Commerce

David Martin
Nielsen//NetRatings, USA

Introduction
(Internet Measurement Industry)

The idea of panel-based Internet audience measurement was a child of the late 1990s "dot-com" era, where financial analysts hinged predictions of stock price rise or ruin on Website rankings. Bold marketing schemes led to spikes in traffic to Websites, which in turn led to higher rankings and the potential for greater advertising revenues. Monthly rankings became as common a mention in company press releases as any other measure of revenue or profit. Despite the sudden and calamitous collapse of the "new economy" in the second quarter of 2000, Internet audience measurement remains a highly relevant industry.

Figure 1: Top 10 Web Properties (March 2003)

Rank	Web Parent	Top Web Brand	Unique Audience (000)	Q4 2002 Revenue $ (000,000)
1	AOL Time Warner	AOL	94,545	11,320
2	Microsoft	MSN	92,392	8,541
3	Yahoo!	Yahoo!	80,986	286
4	U.S. Government	U.S. Dept. of Defense	46,782	n/a
5	Google	Google	42,903	n/a
6	eBay	eBay	37,349	414
7	RealNetworks	Real	37,180	46
8	Amazon	Amazon	36,015	1,429
9	About-Primedia	About Network	34,613	n/a
10	Terra Lycos	Lycos Networks	33,596	198*

Source: Nielsen//NetRatings, Hoovers Online, Terra Lycos, 2003
*Terra Lycos revenue figures converted from Euros.

The companies operating the top 10 Web parents produced in excess of $20 billion in revenue during the fourth quarter of 2002 (see Figure 1). Combined, those top 10 parents reached 122.8 million unique Internet users during March 2003, or 91% of the active Internet universe.

Relevance has not ebbed, and growth of the Internet universe did not fall victim to the dot-com induced economic flameout of 2000, as Nielsen//NetRatings has recorded a steady rise in the number of both at-home and at-work Internet users. July 2000 saw nearly 144 million home users and just over 34 million work users in the United States (see Figure 2). Those numbers have since grown to more than 174 million and nearly 47 million, respectively, in March 2003.

With the arrival of the Internet and World Wide Web as mainstream media and important commercial vehicles, high-quality, timely and comprehensive data based on user activity and advertising have become vital to businesses, government organiza-

Figure 2: Growth of the Online Universe

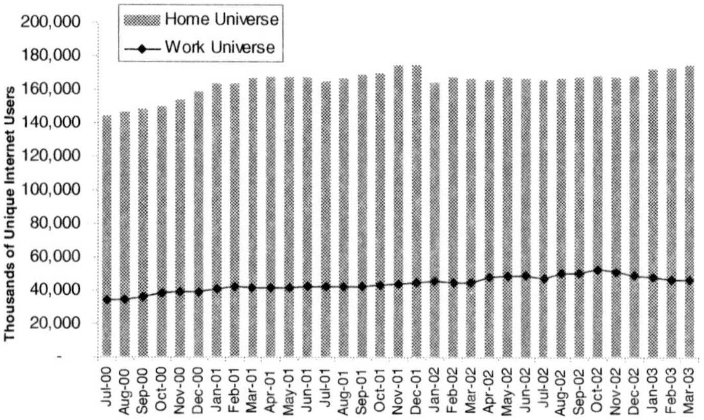

Source: *Nielsen//NetRatings, 2003*
Excludes Internet applications.

tions and other groups using the Internet to reach audiences and customers around the corner and around the globe. Using industry-accepted, proven methods for creating representative research panels and unique measuring technology, Nielsen//NetRatings provides the industry with accurate and reliable information about how people are using the Internet.

The online advertising industry also continues to surprise pundits with its slow but steady rise from the ashes of the dot-com heyday. Throughout 2000 and 2001, small upstart companies that once provided the backbone of ad revenues to Website publishers, first pulled their ads and then pulled the plug on their businesses when investor skepticism mounted and venture capital fizzled. A strange thing happened during that time, however, as large traditional business model advertisers began to take a keen interest in the prospects of online advertising. Perhaps as a result of snapping up dying dot-coms to bolster their "interactive" business strate-

Figure 3: Fortune 500 Online Advertising Growth (January through December 2002)

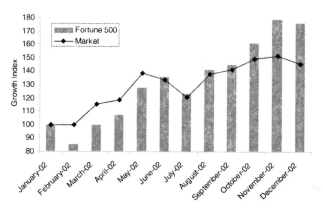

Source: Nielsen//NetRatings, 2003

gies, or perhaps as a result of more mature effectiveness metrics, many Fortune 500 companies expanded their online activities (see Figure 3). Thus, the business of monitoring online advertising activities remains a huge part of the Internet measurement business.

Online advertising was experiencing lean times during the period from 2000 to 2001, but a quiet revolution was taking place. Not only did more viable companies jump into the mix, the ads themselves evolved. The 468 by 60 pixel "banner" may well go down in history as the icon of the childhood of online advertising, but it proved to be the bane of websites trying desperately to prove that online ads were effective. After several years of saturation by the omnipresent banner, World Wide Web users simply became blind to them. Rather than abandon a medium with an ever-growing reach, marketers, who still had cash in their pockets, took to more complex online ad technologies. Such ads, enabled by Flash and Java technologies, can take over one's browser to show a movie

Figure 4: Growth of Rich Media Online Ad Technologies (January 2002 through January 2003)

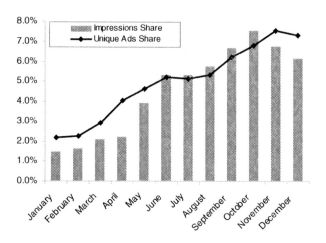

Source: Nielsen//NetRatings, 2003

preview, automatically pop up a new window, and even transpose a TV commercial into a Web page. These technologies have come to be known as "rich media" by the online advertising community, and rich media usage has grown by leaps and bounds in the past few years (see Figure 4).

In 2003, all signs point to growth. The online universe continues its expansion, and large traditional advertisers are jumping into the mix to target their audiences online. More and more companies are demonstrating that they have learned from the highs and lows of the late 1990s "new economy" boom, and in this lies the need for accurate, timely, and detailed information and data solutions.

Methodology of Audience Measurement

The foundation for Nielsen//NetRatings' audience information is methodologies used consistently around the world to create and manage representative research panels. Through strategic partnerships with Nielsen Media Research and ACNielsen, and alliances with leading national and regional market research companies, Nielsen//NetRatings provides its customers with high-quality Internet user activity information that enables decision-makers to understand how people are using the Internet. The data enable Internet players to find ways to better use the Internet to expand their reach and scope of their businesses as well as understand how their competitors are using the medium to gain a strategic advantage. For more than 50 years, advertisers, media planners, content providers and distributors have relied on verifiable behavioral data as the basis for crucial advertising and marketing decisions. Across all media — print, radio, and TV — information has been derived from representative samples under established and accepted rules. The Nielsen//NetRatings service was the first to bring these accepted methods of audience research to the Internet, the fastest growing medium of all time.

Today, using Nielsen//NetRatings data, decision-makers are able to base critical decisions regarding Internet content and advertising delivery wholly, or in part, upon high-quality sample-based research. The primary goal of high-quality, sample-based research is to construct a panel that mirrors the population it aims to represent, so that the information gathered from the sample group accurately reflects the behavior of the larger population. Critical components of any sample-based research service are enumeration, sample design, and sample management. A representative sample is dependant on such factors as sample recruiting and cooperation rates, sample management, and accurate projections to the larger population.

Around the world, Nielsen//NetRatings conducts an independent, continuous enumeration process that delivers the most current estimates of the online population. Each month, Nielsen//NetRatings constructs a random sample using a Random Digit Dial (RDD) approach, and conducts interviews to determine the current level of Internet access at home and in the workplace as well as household and workplace demographics. This information is compared to current national information, such as Census Bureau information in the United States, to estimate Internet penetration among each country's national population. It is important to have up to date enumeration studies, as this information is applied to the sample data to project audiences for the at-home panel, at-work panel, as well as local market and regional reports. Outdated estimates fail to reflect current online audience size and composition and will yield misleading information on site traffic.

For a sample to be representative, the process for recruiting panel members must be random. If the selection process is not random, bias is introduced into the sample, and the information will not reflect the true behavior of the larger population. In other words, nonrandom samples are likely to be skewed toward certain types of Internet users.

The next step is to secure maximum participation from this randomly selected sample. One important indicator of sample quality is the extent to which the recruitment process supports and maximizes cooperation, which is directly tied to how representative the sample is and therefore, how reliable the information from the sample is.

Sample frames for all Nielsen//NetRatings panels worldwide are solidly based on Random Digit Dial (RDD) sampling principles. The sampling procedure for the United States panels select, with equal probability, a random sample from a base of all residential phone numbers in the country. Since households with multiple phone numbers have a higher chance of being included in the panel, these households are identified during the initial recruitment call and their weights are adjusted to take into account their higher probability of being included in the panel.

Based on the sampling frames above, all Nielsen//NetRatings recruitment is conducted by telephone. One key advantage of phone recruitment is that it allows for two-way interaction between the research company and the respondent. This interaction enables the research company to address any questions the respondent may have, thereby ensuring a higher degree of cooperation than one-way mail processes do. Also, to ensure that hard-to-reach individuals are contacted, the calling can be spread over multiple days and also during different times in the day.

For the at-home sample, phone numbers are dialed and con-tacted households are interviewed to identify households eligible to be in the panel (have a PC and Internet access). Eligible households that are recruited to participate in the panel are mailed a member-ship packet including the tracking software and installation instruc-tions, and a toll-free number for technical support. Sending physi-cal copies of the tracking software, as opposed to requesting panelists to download software, minimizes technical issues and ensures maximum installation rates.

Eligible households that decline to participate, as well as households without Internet access and nonresidential phone num-bers are contacted again in subsequent months. Nonworking or non-contacted phone numbers are also attempted again. Thus, repeated attempts are made to ensure that all eligible households are identified, contacted and recruited.

The at-work panel recruitment functions in much the same way as the at-home panel. At-work panel recruitment begins with an original RDD sample representing the universe of United States households. Each household is contacted by phone and respondents over age 16 are asked to participate in the Nielsen//NetRatings Internet research at work. Each individual receives a series of follow-ups by e-mail, mail and by phone in order to maximize cooperation. All respondents are mailed a membership kit containing the tracking software, installation instructions, including a toll-free number for technical support, a reiteration of the requirements for participation and information for their employers. Requirements for participation in the at-work panel include access to a non-shared PC used primarily for work.

An important component to maximizing cooperation rates among recruited panelists is sample management. Panelists are sent a "welcome" email or letter when they first install software to confirm that they have successfully installed the software. A reminder email or phone call is delivered to those recruits who have not yet successfully installed the software. Additionally, those panelists who have installed software but who have never sent data are contacted to determine if panel support is needed. Finally, for those panelists who have successfully installed the software, but who have ceased sending data for a period of 30 days or more, an email and a phone call are deployed to identify whether the panelist is a naturally light surfer or whether there may be technical difficulties.

The actual measurement of Internet activity and retrieval of data have been designed to be as unobtrusive as possible. After installation and completion of a brief demographic profile, panel member households with multiple surfers will see a screen at the beginning of each browser session that asks them to identify the particular active member. This is the only non-transparent measurement from the panel member's perspective. All data are securely and unobtrusively transmitted to Nielsen//NetRatings in real time as the panel member browses the Internet. There is no activity required on the part of the panel members in terms of recording Internet activity or saving or transferring the data collected to Nielsen//NetRatings.

This process is the most rigorous approach to constructing high quality, representative online panels, ensuring the most accurate and reliable information about how people are using the Internet. In the hands of Nielsen//NetRatings audience measurement engineers, data from panelists are then constructed into reports showing the unique audience of Websites and Internet applications by projecting panelists to meet with the enumerated universe. Panelist activity feeds other data points such as time spent on Websites and the number of pages they viewed, as well as the number of surfing sessions people launched in a given time frame. These data end up on the NetRatings client interface on a weekly and monthly basis.

Methodology of Online Ad Tracking

Capturing and measuring online advertising activity is one of the most challenging aspects of Internet measurement. While television advertising has a simple format of 15, 30, or 60-second spots, the nature of the online medium allows advertisers to literally invent new technologies to fit their evolving needs. In seven years, online advertising has evolved from simple banners to ads that use Macromedia's Flash technology to deliver high-quality motion graphics. The creative canvas expanded to include skyscraper ads that climb the side of Web pages and pop-ups and pop-unders that spawn new browser windows. Consumers have become more and more conditioned to online ads, formats such as interstitials (ads that appear between page loads), floating ads (ads that operate on top of a Web page inside the browser window), and streaming ad formats that allow transposition of TV commercials to the Web. In the fourth quarter of 2002, online advertisers utilized more than 14 standardized ad formats and myriad "nonstandard" ones.

Given the evolutionary nature of the online medium, a technology to capture and analyze online advertisements must be adaptable to constant changes in delivery methods, and scalable to the ever-expanding Internet universe. Nielsen//NetRatings' AdRelevance service makes use of a patented technology system, centered on a proprietary intelligent agent called Cloudprober™ to tackle this never-ending process of measurement. This collection of technology is comprised of several major subsystems: traffic analysis, site selection and definition, the Cloudprober™ intelligent agent, automatic ad detection™ classification engine, and data integrity.

Web traffic data is a cornerstone to understanding Web surfer behavior and advertising impressions. One of the most elegant aspects of the Web is the freedom it affords with hyperlinks, allowing Web surfers to effortlessly catapult from site to site by simply clicking a link. Traffic data are a composite record of the URLs requested by individual users as they navigate the Web.

Studying groups of users and the pages they visit yields a picture of the popularity of various sites. Site rankings are extremely important in the Internet economy because more traffic often means more opportunity to generate revenue. For instance, content publishers (websites) can earn money by displaying third party content (advertisements) alongside their content. In short, advertising impressions and spending are inextricably tied to traffic. This is why AdRelevance uses traffic data to determine how often different pages are sampled.

Using robust Web traffic sources, AdRelevance creates a map of Web properties to determine which locations within these sites are the most popular. Once this map is complete the CloudProber goes to work pinging the higher-trafficked Web pages more often than less popular ones in order to accurately represent real-life Internet usage. For example, the CloudProber hits *finance.yahoo.com* far more times than *smallbusiness.yahoo.com*, because the former has about 500 times the page views of the latter. Collecting information from Web pages in such a representative way yields a far more accurate picture of online advertising activity than simple "spidering" methodologies, a system in which computers blindly follow links through a Website with no regard to that link's relevance.

AdRelevance selects the sites it monitors using a vigorous methodology intended to uncover significant and influential online advertising outlets. Criteria for the methodology include traffic, popularity, dominance in a targeted niche market, affiliation with a prominent ad sales network, partnership or ownership by a well-established brand, and material press coverage.

AdRelevance creates definitions for each monitored site to include all pages that share the same branded identity. While many sites consist of a single domain, others span multiple domains or are confined to certain sections of a domain. The result is an extensive and salient list of sites that account for the vast majority of online advertising. AdRelevance currently probes more than 1,100 Web properties, consisting of about 2,500 Web domains, which reach about 88 % of the active online universe of users.

The Cloudprober™ is the intelligent agent component of the AdRelevance technology that autonomously conducts a sample by repeatedly fetching Web pages at variable intervals. This automated sampling system is infinitely more scalable than a human collection system like a clipping service or a panel. Increasing the volume of probes is a simple process compared to recruiting and training more people to perform the same task.

Automated retrieval of Web pages is only a small piece of the puzzle; because most ad content changes or rotates over time, relevant pages must be continuously sampled in the correct proportions to accurately reconstruct the frequency of specific advertisements. Furthermore, due to the sheer size of the Web, sampling algorithms must be finely tuned to optimize the allocation of resources (network bandwidth, database storage, processor time, etc.) and simultaneously enable maximum Internet coverage.

Representative sampling is particularly important in online advertising. Most Web pages have rotating advertisements that vary each time the page is loaded. Due to the size of the Web, definitively determining what happens on each page within a site every time it loads is impossible. A more practical approach is to understand the likelihood that a given ad will appear on any page within a site.

In terms of traffic, not all pages hold equal importance because traffic to each page does not contribute equally to a site's total impressions. The more a page is visited, the more ad impressions that can occur there. This is precisely why the Cloudprober fetches pages with heavy traffic more often than pages with less traffic. Using traffic as a weighting factor yields a representative sample and ultimately leads Cloudprober to mimic the behavior of the real user population. For instance, when traffic shifts from one section of a site to another or from site to site, the Cloudprober adjusts which pages it samples accordingly. The net effect is a timely and relevant sample.

Cloudprober is also equipped to collect geographically targeted ads. Many ad-serving technologies recently developed the ability to target ads at Web users by tracing their IP addresses to specific geographic locales. For instance, a user who connects to an ISP in Atlanta, Georgia might be served a special advertisement for an Atlanta-area auto dealership. In order to collect such ads, the Cloudprober routes its probes through geographic regions in the United States in proportion to the amount of actual traffic coming from each region.

Once the sample is conducted, the data are analyzed to determine how often each ad appears. The expected number of occurrences per page view is an ad's frequency. Multiplying ad frequency by the total page requests made by visitors to the site yields impressions. Finally, multiplying impressions by the rate card value of advertising on the site (usually expressed as a cost per thousand impressions) gives an approximation of spending.

Automatic Ad Detection (AAD) is the component of the AdRelevance technology that identifies and extracts advertising content from the Web pages retrieved by the Cloudprober. First, HTML is cleaned and converted into a hierarchical form known as the Document Object Model so that AdRelevance can analyze the content in precisely the form in which it is provided by servers and rendered by browsers. To ensure that AdRelevance can extract advertisements from page content generated dynamically on the client side (browser), a powerful engine then parses and interprets any JavaScript present in the page. Next, highly tuned heuristics are applied to the document to extract candidate ad fragments. Later, these fragments are analyzed for uniqueness and stored in the database.

The power and flexibility of AAD means that the AdRelevance system is infinitely more scalable than a process that involves humans. Unlike human-based approaches, which tend to be labor-intensive and error-ridden, AAD autonomously and comprehensively identifies and extracts advertisements. Moreover, AdRelevance can easily adapt and extend AAD to handle new forms of advertising, such as rich media, by simply inserting appropriate rules into the system.

AdRelevance puts every collected ad through a rigorous classification system. Each ad first passes through a structural classification process that analyzes its uniqueness. Ads that the system has previously encountered receive an extra tally while new ads create a fresh record in the database. The ad's technology and pixel dimensions are also determined in this phase of classification.

If an ad is new, the system ascertains its click-through destination. This destination URL conveys a tremendous amount of information about the advertiser. To ensure the highest data quality, a highly trained classification specialist reviews every ad to double check the automated classification and adds any missing details. The result is a high-caliber data set that can be queried by a variety of attributes including industry, segment, company, division, brand, product, ad strategy, ad technology, delivery method, and size. This richly detailed AdRelevance taxonomy was developed specifically for online advertising based on the patterns observed in AdRelevance's collection of advertisements, accepted

Figure 5: Nielsen//NetRatings AdRelevance Data Cycle

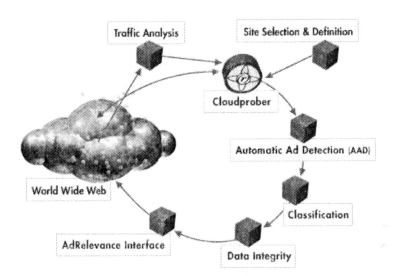

norms from traditional advertising, and feedback from charter customers.

When this process (see Figure 5) is complete and data have been quality checked, the result is a weekly update of the AdRelevance system showing all the ads found on sites the system probes. Clients may then use the Web interface to build queries based on company hierarchy, website genre or property, ad technology or size, delivery mechanism such as pop-up or pop-under, and ad strategy. The true power of the AdRelevance system becomes apparent when using the report builder. The client has the ability to essentially construct a query and filter by virtually any attribute in the system.

The level of sophistication that clients wish to achieve when utilizing the resources of NetRatings' Client Analytics department becomes clear when we see that so much can be achieved with just the syndicated product. A client can find all the advertisers on a particular Website, or on a particular genre of Websites such as sports or news sites. If the client wants, he or she can build a custom list of sites and find all the advertisers on that list, or the client can flip it around and find all the sites upon which an advertiser or group of advertisers placed their ads. The client can view metrics in terms of ad impressions, the number of times an ad was rendered for viewing on a Web page, rate card value, the estimated price an advertiser would pay for those ads, or unique ads and the number of unique ad creatives.

The Business Model of Client Analytics

As the Internet economy has matured, clients have become more sophisticated in their research needs. Syndicated services such as NetView and AdRelevance provide vital "ready-to-go" metrics that are used on a daily basis, but when clients want to answer a specific question in more detail, they need a custom touch. The Nielsen//NetRatings Client Analytics department addresses the needs of high-profile clients that want to explore online measurement databases beyond the capabilities of Nielsen//NetRatings' syndicated services.

The massive amount of panelist click-stream data that exist in the Neilsen//NetRatings database requires a careful set of well-designed syndicated reports to maximize the information available while keeping the amount of processing time reasonable and recognizing storage limitations. Examples of these syndicated reports include top line metrics of well-defined Web properties such as unique audience, page views, time spent on sites, and reach in the Internet universe. Web category analysis has also become very popular, where clients compare their properties to others in well-defined categories and subcategories of the World Wide Web, such as search engines, email providers, and retail shopping sites. Demographic analysis is a huge part of the NetView syndicated service, in which clients can break out sites and categories by well-established demographic breaks including age, income, household size, education, gender, race, and others. Performing a search for sites that skew heavily to particular demographic targets is also made available in the service. Clients also use NetRatings tools to figure out the common audience of disparate Web properties, connection speeds of people visiting sites, and unduplicated audience numbers of custom groupings of sites.

The AdRelevance service provides an even higher degree of flexibility with its on-the-fly report building structure. Clients can analyze a site's advertisers by company, division, brand, or product, or they can group advertisers on a site by industry or industry segment. With the ability to group by more than one system attribute, clients can perform such analyses like this over time, receiving real-time data showing advertisers on a site grouped by month and then by their industry or another attribute. Clients can run competitive analyses by filtering to particular advertisers and then determining upon which sites those advertisers are buying ads. Website publishers use the tool to find out which clients are signing on with competing sites, and if a competing site has adopted a new advertising technology. Furthermore, with services such as AdAlert™, clients can automatically be notified via email if a new advertiser has shown up on a competing site, or if a competing advertiser has placed a new ad in the most recent week.

Despite the immense offerings of the Nielsen//NetRatings syndicated measurement services, highly sophisticated clients are always in need of more dynamic and customized data runs that are simply not feasible to provide on a regular basis. Instead of charging clients additional cash every time they want a new custom report, Nielsen//NetRatings sales account managers sell custom research credits to any interested client. These credits are purchased in bulk as part of a client's contract, and then can be later redeemed for custom services. This method of selling custom research affords the client the ability to breathe easy when they need an answer to an urgent question. Instead of going through the contract process of proposing a custom data run and having it faxed around for signatures, the client simply requests data at a cost of credits. This credit-based process also produces salient metrics describing department activities, in which managers can monitor how many credits a client "burns" in a certain period, and how much research effort is expended per credit redeemed.

Some clients thus purchase Neilsen//NetRatings syndicated services to answer the bulk of their queries, and then purchase and redeem research credits to fill in the holes of any questions that cannot be immediately answered by the services. Other clients purchase the syndicated services and use them religiously, but then go far beyond by purchasing large blocks of credits and even custom-contracted projects to answer complex questions.

Several examples of audience measurement custom reports underline the complexity of the questions being asked by clients. Many want to know what audience data look like when certain Web properties or pages are grouped together in ways that lie outside the prescribed data dictionary. An example of this type of report is a client who wants to know how many people saw the combined pages of *www.somesite.com/sports/baseball* and *www.othersite.com/sports/baseball.* Perhaps they want to define a unique universe of users who frequent a particular set of Websites and pages. Another example of custom audience measurement data is to follow users of a certain page or site and track their behavior within a specified time period before and after visiting the page. This type of report is called a Website "source/loss" report, because it displays visitation behavior based on time spent before visiting a Website and after the visitor moves on to a new site. This type of analysis can yield highly different results than simply analyzing referring Website links. A Website owner may know that much of his or her traffic is referred from *www.widgets.com* but doesn't know that within five minutes of visiting his site, most of his users *visit www.findawidget.com* and *www.searchforwidgets. com,* where the Website owner has no referring links.

Another type of custom information sought by clients involves targeting particular panelist behavior over a long period of time. Clients sometimes desire to define a sub-panel of users who display a particular behavior over a long period of time such as four to six months, and then analyze what those people do in the most recent month. A useful application of this is to flag anyone who downloads a particular item in the past six months, and then figure out what their favorite Websites are in the most recent month, broken out by demographics. This sort of information provides businesses with actionable data that can accurately describe the users of their products over time, something that can prove or disprove the effectiveness of a product or initiative.

Custom data runs for online advertising are often linked to ad sales. One of the most popular custom AdRelevance reports is called the "lead factory", in which clients receive contact information merged with ad impressions and spending estimates. One lead factory report displays the top 50 advertisers in each of the United

States along with the number of ads, their predominant strategy, their most-used ad technology, and contact information. This gives an ad sales force the immediate ability to call a potential client and know exactly what types of creative strategies and messaging that advertiser utilizes. Another lead factory report displays a comprehensive list of the newest online advertisers and their contact information. When merged with site information, this sort of analysis can tell an ad sales force everything about a potential client, and can be vital to maintaining a competitive edge.

Another type of custom online advertising report involves custom coding of advertisements by human eyes. Often, clients want to know if ads featuring a certain brand logo or partnership have been seen online. An example of this is the process of flagging desktop computer ads to determine if computer manufacturers attach processor logos onto their creatives. While this type of custom request involves manual work by human coders, the results are very useful, especially over time. Computer chip manufacturers may want to track the rise and fall of particular processor logos on desktop ads as they cycle through newer technologies. They may also seek to monitor their ostensible partners' real-life compliance with branding deals. Use of this type of custom-coding initiative also applies heavily to seasonal advertising analysis, in which clients want to know how much holiday-specific advertising their competitors purchase each year. A distinct trend exists with holiday-themed online ads in the fourth quarter of each year, and the online medium has proved more and more seasonal as the years progress.

Correctly appropriating human skills in the client analytics department is just as important as maintaining a highly rigorous measurement methodology. A cadre of senior analysts who specialize in specific industry verticals handles client interaction with the department. An example of an industry of coverage would be financial services, in which a senior analyst draws upon extensive experience to not only interact with clients but to focus the data analytics efforts of the department. Typically these analysts work with clients and sales account managers to explore avenues of research, create project outlines, and provide a credit cost or price tag for initiatives. These analysts then turn to within the department to muster analytical resources such as database analysts and engineers who mine for the appropriate information.

The Nielsen//NetRatings client analytics department thus requires several distinct groups of talent sets. The senior vertical analysts perform the aforementioned duties of interacting with clients and apply industry-specific expertise to the data mining process. A separate group of data analysts with a smaller amount of client interaction concentrate on mining the databases and providing for timely turnaround of data runs. Instead of being industry-specific, these analysts are technology-specific, and work with sales account managers and senior analysts to deliver data. The sum of these parts is an efficient system in which tracking projects from conception to delivery shows a steady flow from one talent set to another, and back.

Case Studies

Case Study (1): Channel Trends and Descriptive Statistics of Loyal Users

The research department of a large sports news Website approached the Nielsen//NetRatings client analytics department with the goal of tracking specific channels within their sites over the course of thirteen months. Instead of tabulating the results of all panelist activity during each distinct month, the client wished to track the behavior of individual panelists who remained in the panel and active during the thirteen-month period. In essence, they wanted to track the loyalty of an actual subset of people over the course of a year, to find out how seasonality affected their Web traffic and how loyal people really are.

The first reason this request came to the custom department was the high degree of resolution desired on the site level. The syndicate service did not adequately break out different sports and features within the site. An example of such a channel is *sportssite.com/mlb* or *sportssite.com/nfl,* representing Major League Baseball and National Football league content, respectively. The second reason for pursuing this request as a custom report was the necessity of creating a custom panel of individuals who displayed activity online over a 13-month period. With a panel of about 50,000 members, there exists a lot of turnover during the course of a year. Panel management tactics combat this attrition, but the number of people in tabulation 13 months ago who still exist in the panel today is considerably smaller than the whole panel.

The first challenge of this project was to parse out the client's website into distinct channels based on URL strings. In many cases, websites follow very strict rules that allow one to easily determine one area of content from another. An example of this would be having the domain name followed by "/mlb" for baseball or "/nfl" for football, and so forth with other sports. Some sites choose to manage their content in a less human-friendly manner, using long number combinations that are harder to decipher than names. In the case of the client, their site was set up in the intuitive sense, and analysts spent some time and soon came up with a map of about 50 different channels inside the client's site. These channels included all professional sports, college sports for both men and women, Olympic sports and other, less-popular ones. The channels also included exclusive content sections featuring analysts and media personalities who specialize in specific areas. With such a comprehensive map of their site, analysts then sat down with the client and selected 20 of the most popular channels upon which to focus the analysis.

The next step of the project involved defining the sub-panel of active users over the previous 13 months. The business logic for the project mandated that a user did not need to be active in each of the previous 13 months, but that the user had to have been active 13 months prior the current month, and at least one month in between. Using this logic, each month's user base of panelists was compared to those of prior months to flag users that were still in the system, and over time, the panel was whittled down to a range of just over 10,000 users.

With a database of 10,000 qualified panelists in hand, analysts could then begin to aggregate user activity in the normal fashion. The only difference in the aggregation process would be that panelists would be excluded if they did not appear in the custom list. To aggregate activity for one channel during a given month, analysts queried the database for all panelists who saw a particular channel URL, such as *sportssite.com/mlb*. After establishing that list of users, exclusion logic was run against the table of eligible panelists, whittling down the list of valid visitors to the channel. After that, weights for each of the panelists could be applied and then projected out with enumeration statistics to reach a count of the unique audience of "loyal" panelists to that channel. The result of such an analysis was a series of trends that displayed the seasonality of each major channel. Analysts then created an inter-active spreadsheet to leverage charting abilities to allow the client

Figure 6: Interactive Spreadsheet Allowing Trend Comparison

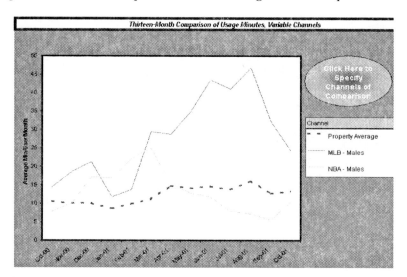

to compare any channel and top-line demographics against each other (see Figure 6).

Now that the analysts established the loyal user base of each custom channel within the client's site, the real analysis of the loyal user base could begin. The most important aspect of this study to the client was to be able to create a demographic profile of usage during each of the 13 months for each channel. The goal of parsing out these metrics by demographics would be to look at seasonal highs and lows and observe changes in the audience composition during these time periods.

Mentioned previously in the audience measurement methodology section, each panelist in the system has a distinct set of demographics associated with him or her. With this set of demographics already in place, it is easy for an analyst to group visitation data by the established demographic breaks of the panelists. This process involves tallying the panelist weights by demographics and projecting them out to an estimate of unique audiences, then doing

Figure 7: Channel-Specific Audience Distributions

	A	B	C	D	E	F
1	Summary					
2	Age Group Distributions					
3	Household Size Distributions					
4	Regional Distributions					
5	Income Bracket Distributions					
6						
7						Summary
8						
9						
10	CHANNEL	MONTH	Total UA	Males	Females	Percent Male
136	Major League Baseball	October-00	2,143,604	1,645,407	498,197	77%
137	Major League Baseball	November-00	1,403,890	1,159,280	244,610	83%
138	Major League Baseball	December-00	1,117,280	863,052	254,228	77%
139	Major League Baseball	January-01	932,709	754,976	177,733	81%
140	Major League Baseball	February-01	1,146,823	924,016	222,807	81%
141	Major League Baseball	March-01	2,161,922	1,696,647	465,275	78%
142	Major League Baseball	April-01	2,738,761	2,000,146	738,615	73%
143	Major League Baseball	May-01	2,408,209	1,721,309	686,900	71%
144	Major League Baseball	June-01	3,070,969	2,381,863	689,106	78%
145	Major League Baseball	July-01	3,431,913	2,724,572	707,341	79%

Source: Nielsen//NetRatings, 2003

the same for usage metrics such as view duration and page views. The final result was an extensive set of descriptive statistics for each channel, with unique audience and usage minutes numbers broken out by age, household size, region, and household income (see Figure 7).

A large sticking point in analyses of demographic information of large scale is that there exists too much data to digest. Thus, the final stage of this analysis was to create custom tools to make researching and using the mined data an easy and intuitive process. Using charting tools and Visual Basic for Applications code in Microsoft Excel, analysts constructed a user interface to display both channel trending information and demographic distribution information for any point in the 13-month time period (see Figure 8). The result was an extremely effective way of putting a friendly face on a large array of raw data, making it easy for researchers in the client's company to come to conclusions about their loyal user base.

Figure 8: Combined Trends and Interactive Distribution View

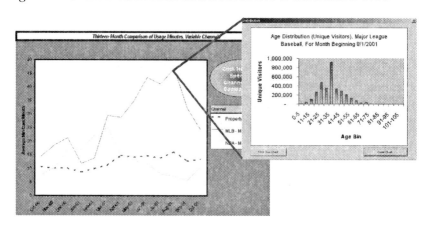

This case demonstrates the necessity of all layers of the custom analytics department, from senior analysts who scope out costs and drive the direction of inquiry to technically skilled analysts who specialize in mining databases and creating custom user interfaces to the data. The culmination of this effort was a series of deliverables that helped the client answer very specific questions about their loyal user base during different points in sports seasons. This information could then be used to drive targeted online advertising sales by demonstrating the affinity of a particular market segment.

Case Study (2): Ad Server Analysis

We mentioned before that the AdRelevance database and client interface afford a high degree of flexibility to create many types of reports. This is true to a large extent, but some information still resides behind the client interface that cannot be syndicated in a reasonable fashion. One such case is when clients wish to know what ad servers online advertisers employ to post their ads. Inquiries of this nature usually come from agencies and ad servers who want to feed their sales force with very specific information about potential or existing clients. The nature of online advertising is such that many major online advertisers use several different ad serving companies to deliver their online messages. This is usually because advertisers desire to promote their products across different networks of sites that utilize different servers. If you want to advertise on a site or network of sites or through a particular agency, you often must accept their advertising procedures.

When the AdRelevance intelligent agent technology, Cloudprober™ records an instance of an online ad, it records information from where that ad was served. This information consists of a long string of often several different URLs from several different servers, because rarely does an ad simply go from one server to the requesting Web page. Intermediate servers act as counters and providers of specific frames of code in which the ads themselves reside. Determining which ad server actually provided the ad creative is sometimes a tricky task, as an ad request from a Web page can bounce around several different servers. Unique online ads can have many different ad servers in the same time period, depending upon the preferences of the site or network. These complexities prevent the AdRelevance service from including ad server information as part of its syndicated delivery of data. Too few clients have expressed interest in paying for the development of such a product through increases in contract value.

When individual clients request such data, the client analytics department steps in to conduct custom analysis using distinct business logic conceived through meetings between analysts, sales people and clients. In this case the client wanted to see the top 500 online advertisers broken out by which ad servers they used. Then they wanted these data linked to our ad contact database in order to provide their sales force with intelligence regarding potential leads. The data mining process for this project was to be used to generate business rather than to answer a specific question or come to a strategic decision.

The business rules agreed upon by the analysts and the client specified that the relevant ad server for a particular instance of an ad on a site would be either the first or second server appearing in the host chain. If only one server existed in the chain, then that was the relevant server. If two or more servers existed in the chain, then the second server in the chain was the relevant one. As a company that provided ad-serving products, the client was confident that following this logic would yield satisfactory results.

The first step in aggregating the ad server data was to combine all the daily ad fetch data into one large table that could then be scaled down into a list of distinct ad server chains. This process requires database packages designed to create large tables out of many smaller tables, then to create an even smaller table by selecting only those values that were distinct. If the Cloudprober fetched an ad from a site multiple times, this entry could leave several identical server chains in the raw data. The resulting tables gave analysts a view of ads and their distinct server chains.

The next step in the process was to perform business logic on the server chains themselves, parsing them and singling out one particular relevant server for the study. This involved a simple program run within the database to search the stings of data for the number of distinct servers and then extract only the relevant one. A single-server string would be easy to identify, but in the case of a long string, the second server would be extracted.

With a list of ads and servers, data could be rolled up under company hierarchies to produce the desired report (see Figure 9). By tabulating impressions data with the unique servers, the resulting set of data showed the relative use of one ad server over

Figure 9: Ad Server Report Example

Overall Rank	Company	Embedded Server	Content Server	Server Impressions
1	Amazon.com, Inc.	ar.atwola.com	ar.atwola.com	6,634,908,777
1	Amazon.com, Inc.			1,871,796,207
1	Amazon.com, Inc.		image.i1img.com	1,204,040,719
1	Amazon.com, Inc.		my.netzero.net	675,881,860
1	Amazon.com, Inc.		my.juno.com	507,667,153
1	Amazon.com, Inc.		i1img.com	389,176,429
1	Amazon.com, Inc.	home.iwon.com	image.i1img.com	227,273,400
1	Amazon.com, Inc.		di.image.eshop.msn.com	160,204,088
1	Amazon.com, Inc.		global.msads.net	110,270,722
1	Amazon.com, Inc.		www.bartleby.com	67,490,732

another. Analysts then merged contact information with ad server information to provide the final product: a comprehensive list of ad server usage in a given time period by the most important online advertisers.

Case Study (3): "Non-Retention" Analysis of Audience Panel Subset

A useful metric in the world of panel-based audience measurement is retention; or of the unique audience that visited a particular Web location last month, how many of those same people visited this month? This information is mission critical to e-commerce Web properties that seek to build a large and loyal client base. A large problem for today's Web retailers is that with the plethora of Websites offering rock-bottom prices and fast shipping, sticking with the same retailer time after time does not necessarily pay off. Retention analysis can thus offer deep insights into the successes or failures of marketing schemes, pricing, or site accessibility.

Nielsen//NetRatings NetView clients enjoy retention reports on a syndicated basis. They can query a particular month and a particular panel, home or work, and learn that Amazon.com retained 51.9% of its previous month's user base from February to March of 2003 and then compare that to their own rates. While most clients find their questions answered at this point, the more sophisticated research departments always look at the data from the positive and negative angles. A complex question that stems from the above simple figures is, "if Amazon retained half of its users month-over-month, where did the other half go?" This question is a perfect candidate for a client analytics department database inquiry.

We have already mentioned the idea of a "sub-panel", or the process of flagging a group of people in the active audience measurement panel that display a particular behavior over a period of time. A client recently approached the department seeking information on where previous users of a particular Web channel went when they abandoned that channel in the next month. The idea here was to establish a pattern of behavior in two consecutive months, based on URL strings that the panelist sees, and then compare the two sub-panels to identify those who dropped out of the sub-panel in the second month. The Web surfing behavior of that very select group of sub-panel dropouts would then be analyzed for the month that they disappeared and the client would have an idea of where their users went when they jumped ship.

The more focused this sort of analysis is, the easier it is to perform. Analysts in this case worked with the client to determine what Internet population they wished to analyze. As is often the case in Internet audience measurement, Website owners and researchers often have very specific competitors in mind when focusing their analyses. Analysts discovered in this case that the client wanted to know which major search Websites their non-retained users visited in consecutive months. This meant that the construction of the sub-panel would involve flagging all panelists that visited the client's search site and then comparing that list to those who visited their site the following month. The resulting discrepancies were then turned into a list of panelists who abandoned the client's search site from the previous month.

Instead of taking that list and aggregating a report of all of those non-retained users' Web activities, analysts could focus on finding out whether or not those users showed up on any of their competitors' sites. If a panelist did not show up on a competitor's the next month, analysts could check to see if the panelist showed up at all in the active panel for that month. If the panelist registered no activity that month, then analysts would conclude that the user abandoned all activity on the entire competitive set, not only the client's. The other case would be that the panelist might have dropped out of the panel under measurement for the newest month. Keeping track of these panelists is important in such a study, as panel attrition can potentially mask real trends.

The final product of this custom study was a report showing the unique audience in one month that appeared on the client's site and then of that audience that did not show up, how large of an audience they formed on competing sites.

Case Study (4): Where the Ad Dollars Go

The Nielsen//NetRatings AdRelevance service was created under the premise that advertisers want to know how they stack up against their competition and Website publishers want to know what kind of clients their competition retains. The extensive flexibility of the AdRelevance report builder allows both sides, media buyers and media sellers, to create an amazing array of analyses to this end. Clients can filter to specific ad attributes, industries, Web genres, or creative technologies and find out how the competition is using the myriad technologies of the online medium to reach consumers.

Similar to the case of user "non-retention" mentioned in the last case study, sometimes AdRelevance clients are more interested in the clients they and their competitors are not retaining over time. The problem with this type of question is that in order to build a set of reports to answer your questions, you have to have some idea of who or what you are looking for in the system. A Web publishing client can use the report builder to track their competition's client base and compare it to their own, but it is hard to find the most important clients when querying a database containing thousands of sites and tens of thousands of companies.

Database expertise comes in very handy when clients want to search for a specific answer to a very general question such as, "of the most important clients in online advertising today, which ones am I missing?" Much like the non-retention analysis of unique audiences, this type of project requires the creation of a subset of companies in the AdRelevance database to query against the larger dataset.

The first approach to this problem could be to create a list of all the companies that advertise on the client's site in a given time period and then run top client reports on all other competing websites, excluding those companies. This would produce a report that tells the client all the clients unique to competing Websites. Analysts could then merge these data with ad contact information and produce a tidy list of leads.

The problem with the above scenario is that this sort of analysis can be performed using the syndicated service and some spreadsheet savvy, and it does not necessarily answer the question of which of the client's non-advertisers are the most important. Working with the client to establish what types of companies are important often leads to external data sources that rank companies by metrics other than ad impressions. The most frequently mentioned measure of company importance is the Fortune 500. Importing Fortune 500 data into the AdRelevance database and then filtering custom reports of potential clients by this distinguishing trait yields a far more salient list of leads.

The fun does not stop there, when one considers that any outside source of company information can be imported into the database. As online advertising has matured over the last three years, the importance of the leading advertisers across traditional media has grown. The first question that any industry analyst asks about the online medium is whether or not big-budget marketers are spending more of their ad dollars online. The answer to this question is yes, and the next question is always, "where are they putting their ads?" Clients want to know this exact same thing, and can leverage the power of custom analytical services to cut online advertising data with metrics that identify the top advertisers across all media. An example of this type of data run was to combine the cross-media reporting power of Nielsen's Monitor Plus service with the AdRelevance database. Monitor Plus provided a list of the top 100 advertisers across all media over the past few years, and custom analysts coded these lists to create a custom grouping of AdRelevance-tracked advertisers. As mentioned above, once such a list is compiled in the database, the sky is the limit in terms of figuring out where these advertisers go online, and which sites they avoid.

Case Study (5): Internet User Segmentation and Affinity

Internet media buyers ultimately want consumers to purchase more of their products and services. Unfortunately, converting Internet ad placements to cold, hard cash is trickier than simply noting a correlation between a spike in ad impressions and an increase in Website traffic and hoping for the best. A marketer's dollars are better spent when he or she understands a specific series of behaviors behind the audience he is reaching. While most Websites can say they reach a particular niche audience, marketers love to go beyond the demographics and understand consumer behavior. It does not matter if you serve ads to your target audience if none of them spend money in your market.

One of the best ways to understand consumer behavior using Internet audience measurement is to segment Internet users into categories based on surfing traits, and to analyze these segments as subsets of the Internet universe. An example of this type of segmentation would be to divide up a site's users into people who visit frequently, moderately, or infrequently. Alternately, you can divide visitors of a group of sites into similar strata, to better understand usage of a Web genre. A few surfing traits that differentiate Internet users are the time they spend online, the number of times they visit a particular site in a given period, the number of pages they view, or any of these usage metrics focused inside particular areas of a site, such as secure https mode.

Secure mode usage is an important proxy for Web sales conversion for retailers and account usage for banks. While confounding factors such as shopping cart abandonment and last-minute cold feet muddy the waters in determining dollars spent, being able to identify Web surfers who spend a significantly greater amount of time in secure mode is invaluable.

Marketers know that the individuals that make up a target audience are not all alike, or even equal. Some spend a lot of time browsing a website, while others who spend less time online end up actually buying more. These two groups are not necessarily the same people. A good example scenario involves a DVD movie retailer seeking to target its online advertising in a way that not only reaches a target audience of DVD buffs, but specifically finds the subset of movie fans that spend money online frequently, or at least spend a lot of time in secure transaction mode on retail sites. This problem can be broken down into two main questions that the DVD retailer wants answered. The first is, "what do serious movie fans look like online?" The second is, "who are the ones spending money online, and where can I target them?"

Finding the right demos of heavy movie fans:

- Create a relevant basket of movie information sites.
- Segment users of those sites into heavy, medium, and light users.
- Project demographic information for each stratum.
- Perform audience composition indices on demographics against average users.
- Single out high audience composition indices for further analysis into secure mode behavior.
- Perform audience "affinity" analysis to determine cross-visitation behavior.

The most logical place to seek out an audience for DVD advertising is on movie information and fan sites. Such sites could include data repositories such as imdb.com, review sites such as Entertainment Weekly or rottentomatoes.com, or movie and studio-specific portals. Creating a pool of these types of hangouts is the first step to narrowing down the movie buff's online behavior.

The next step is to utilize audience segmentation analysis to separate users of these sites into different classes. The simplest example is to assign each user a label of heavy, medium, or light depending upon whether or not they meet or exceed a particular usage threshold. If you segment by average time spent on the basket of sites per month, at one polar extreme you will observe users who spend lots of time researching movies, reading reviews, searching for pictures and biographies of stars and other information. At the other end you will see users who give reviews a cursory glance, seek local show times, and then head to the theaters. This audience may be better segmented by visitation frequency, defined as the average number of unique sessions (30 minute blocks of time) users spend on a site in a given month. Using visitation instead of time can eliminate bias towards the heavy readers, but then assumes that the amount of time a person spends researching movies is irrelevant to the marketer.

After segmentation is complete, standard audience measurement and demographic analysis can be applied to the samples using established methods of weights and projections. The most important metric in the resulting demographic analysis will be the audience demographic composition index constructed by comparing the demographic makeup of the segmented audience to that of the average Internet audience makeup. These indices may show that a heavy Internet movie buff audience will have an 18 to 24 year old component, 1.6 times greater than an average Internet audience. It may also show persons between the age of 25 and 34 index high, but not quite as high as the younger set. The analyst can then proceed down the list of demographics that includes age, gender, occupation, education, and household income, among others, and pick out extremely high indices.

The next question is how behavioral traits such as high visitation to movie sites compare to transactional behavior, specifically frequency of secure mode visitations to retail sites. Do the same users who appear to be big movie fans also buy movies online? Is it worth giving up on one demographic and focusing on another? Taking the same sub-sample of heavy movie site fans and tracking their behavior inside secure transaction sites can address these questions. The easiest way to perform this is to create a basket of relevant secure retail sites and construct demographic profiles of those heavy movie visitors with respect to audience composition. Such sites could include amazon.com, NetFlix, Barnes & Noble, DVD.com, even eBay. Putting the indices side-by-side may yield some insight into which visitors the DVD marketer should be targeting (see Figure 10).

Note that in the above example, the audience that indexed the highest over the average audience was persons between 18 and 24, the college set. The next category, persons between 25 and 34, indexed slightly lower, and the 35 to 49 year-olds were close to a normal audience. The marketer now knows that while the college age people have a high affinity with movie sites, they index lower in visits to transaction modes. The next age group up, however, indexes far higher in the transaction mode on the basket of relevant

Figure 10: Comparing Audience Composition and Transaction Indices

Demographic	Movie Fan Index	Transaction Index
Age 2 – 11	85	2
Age 12 – 17	92	23
Age 18 – 24	160	84
Age 25 – 34	145	198
Age 35 – 49	102	135

retail sites. This is what the marketer is looking for: a qualified audience with money to spend and proven buying habits.

The last piece of the puzzle is to perform source-loss and site and application cross-usage analysis to determine if there are any specific niche sites and applications that the targeted groups frequent. Source-loss analysis tells you where a person visited before and after visiting a specific Website. The analyst can set a specific time period in which to track source and loss, usually within two to five minutes before and after a particular visit. Site affinity analysis tells you the most popular Websites visited by a sub-panel of people. Application cross-usage analysis can tell you what desktop applications a particular user spends a lot of time using.

Figure (11) shows that in an example scenario, the highly prized demographic visited major portals and shopping sites within two minutes of using movie information sites. This information, when expanded to hundreds of sites, can be used to create a targeted ad-purchasing pattern.

Figure (12) lends some explanation for why the college set, despite having such an affinity with movie sites online, does not

Figure 11: Loss Sites of User Sub-Panel (Demographic: Persons Age 25 – 34, Heavy Movie Site Affinity)

Loss Site	Loss Traffic %
msn.com	25
yahoo.com	23
amazon.com	10
Netflix.com	8
ebay.com	3

Figure 12: Top Application Usage of User Sub-Panel (Demographic: Persons Age 18-24, Heavy Movie Site Affinity)

Application	Percent of Traffic
Microsoft Office	25
Internet Explorer	23
Kazaa	10
AIM	8
MSN Messenger	3

index as high on the spending side. Perhaps they are utilizing high-speed connections and file-sharing software to download movies instead of going to theaters or buying DVDs.

The moral of this story is that when employing Internet user segmentation, the results of one finding can drive the implementation of other methods. In this case, we sought to run affinity and cross-usage analyses on very specific demographic groups after we determined that they had some value to further investigate. It also showed us that while a group may demonstrate a particularly desirable behavior such as spending a lot of time on movie sites, they might not have a proclivity towards actually buying a product.

Role of Client Analytics in the Future

The success of the client analytics department over the recent past should not be viewed in a vacuum. The products that the client analytics department delivers are extensions of the extensive and comprehensive product that appears on the syndicated Nielsen// NetRatings services each week. Perhaps the single greatest "new" aspect of the product that custom data analysts bring to the table is the ability to add value to existing data through industry-specific expertise and familiarity with the more technological aspects of the data set. As clients become familiar and comfortable with custom data requests that become common, the idea that those data cuts appear on the syndicated service as either prepackaged reports or searchable results becomes more appealing. In that sense, the department fits in with the goals of product development and enhancement. Client analytics will always be on the front line of client-driven innovation, because the custom analysts are the ones answering the questions that cannot be answered with existing syndicated products.

Some products that are easily produced by "canned" scripts that merely adjust date properties but query the same information are great candidates for syndication. The AdRelevance lead factory reports are a good example of this, where producing a new section of the AdRelevance Website that offers lead factory results for particular sites or states or Web genres would be relatively simple. The only drawback in the case of syndicating a report such as the lead factory is that many clients would lose interest in a product that they know all other clients have. Part of the appeal of the lead factory is that one pays a premium for data that other clients cannot easily produce with the syndicated service. The client analytics department can charge a premium for such a report because it affords a great competitive advantage, and not enough clients buy the report to spread the cost around. If the product were to be offered in the syndicated service, the cost per client, and perhaps even the value afforded to each client, would be drastically reduced.

On the audience measurement side, a good candidate for syndication may be a rollup of particular URLs that indicate popular search engine terms. Clients may eventually want to know the unique audience, page views, and time that Web users spend searching for the most popular search terms on particular sites. Another good candidate for conversion from custom to syndicated is the source/loss analysis, in which we specify the top Websites visited by users within a certain time period before and after they visit a particular site. The large problem with syndicating a metric like that is the massive amount of processing required to determine source/loss information for just one site. Doing such a thing for every site Nielsen//NetRatings reports on is an impossibility given the limits of technology. As time goes by and processing power and storage become cheaper, such enormous reports may end up in syndication.

Even without technological barriers to syndication, some questions will always be better answered through custom work. Specific page rollups to determine unique audience and other top-line metrics of obscure combinations of URLs will always be something best done on a case-by-case basis. Such reports are often connected with a very specific business question, such as finding out how many people downloaded a particular item in a given week, or how much time people spent reading a particular set of news articles by the same author.

Segmentation analyses of websites based on demographic breaks will also always remain in the custom corner. However, the results of these segmentations may point the product development team towards trends in Internet usage that may have gone unnoticed. Isolating important demographic groups that display certain behaviors online could lead to syndicated reports featuring the behavior of extremely targeted groups. Seasonality displayed by sports fans, for example, could lead to syndicated reports on sports properties and sports advertisers that adjust for the time of year, helping clients recognize and adjust for seasonality on the Internet and opening doors for further custom analysis.

Keeping a finger on the pulse of the client is an important job in an organization that consistently has to adjust for the torrid pace of Internet evolution. Technological advances require constant definitional changes to even the most basic syndicated services, but the sophistication of the client base is only uncovered through one-on-one interaction with research departments. The Nielsen// NetRatings client analytics department will continue to use its business model not only to mine audience measurement and advertising databases to answer client questions, but also to discover emerging realities in consumer behavior and new research possibilities.

Editor's Notes

E-commerce strategic initiatives continue to evolve as innovative technologies facilitate new and faster ways of communicating content from organizations to the marketplace via the Internet. In order to enhance online activities however, decision-makers need to better understand the behavior of their customers, whether they are businesses or private consumers. This past chapter illustrated how advanced search, query and reporting techniques along with data mining methodologies enable organizations to extract meaningful information from the vast terabytes of "real-time" data that exist in the e-commerce environment. With this information they can further enhance online strategic initiatives to ultimately provide consumers with a higher valued mechanism to gain insights, obtain services and purchase products.

The final chapter of this book will shift focus considerably from advertising to address one of the most complex industries due to its structural transformation. The utilities industry includes a number of factors that introduce risk for providers of energy. The following material will illustrate both the complexities involved in the process of providing energy to consumers and how quantitative methods can help decision-makers better manage the risks involved in doing so.

Chapter X

Taking a Close Look at the Evolving Utilities Industry:

Factors That Drive Volatility and Methods to Help Manage It

Nicholas Galletti
Con Edison Energy, USA

Background on the Evolution of the Utilities Industry

The electric industry has undergone a radical transformation over the last five years. Prior to the late 1990s, the industry was heavily regulated. Investor-owned utility companies operated in franchise areas, under an agreement with local regulators that no competitors would be allowed, in exchange for the utility to pass through all prudently incurred costs of serving its customers as well as an allowed rate of return for required capital investments. This system worked reasonably well for decades.

Volatility in the Supply and Demand of Electricity

In the early 1990s, a combination of economic recession and aggressive building of generation plants resulted in a surplus of generation (in the electric industry, the amount of capacity surplus is measured as "reserve margin", calculated as total supply divided by total demand). As a result, wholesale market prices fell. Under the regulatory system in place, rates were established such that utilities could recover all of the generation related costs, which included all fixed and variable costs, inclusive of the excess capacity. Such rates would sometimes contain a fuel adjuster to allow for a pass-through of costs as spot prices changed. Price risk was thus borne by consumers or "rate-payers".

Under this regime, price volatility was not a major concern. Generally, wholesale transactions were priced at a level closely resembling variable cost of production. Besides regulations on such pricing, there was also no incentive to charge any more, as utility profits were regulated and "excess" profitability would be returned to ratepayers anyway.

It was not long before large customers began noticing the discrepancies between the rates they paid (which were based on average costs and included all fixed as well as sunk capital costs) and the lower marginal prices observed in the spot market. Rates were higher still due to carrying the costs of the excess capacity being spread over the same number of Megawatt-hours (MWhs) in determining rates, perversely causing rates to be higher under conditions of generation surplus. Some began demanding discounts under the threat of moving out of the service territory (they could not seek alternate suppliers within the same service territory). At around the same time, independent generators, who recently had been allowed to build plants and sell their output to the incumbent utilities, were eager to find new customers.

Deregulation

As a result, these large customers forced the industry to begin the process of deregulation. The process involved all of the stakeholders (customers, independent generators, regulators, investors, etc.), and lasted until the latter part of the 1990s. This resulted in the creation of independent system operators (ISOs), which were charged with running the power system without favoring any entity. Generators and load (the electric industry typically uses the term "load" to represent customer usage or demand) were to submit bids and offers for power into the market, and market prices would replace a cost-based regulated pricing structure. In theory, market prices would send proper price signals to either build more generation and/or reduce usage, ultimately creating a more efficient system. Also, customers were gradually allowed to choose alternate suppliers.

The promise was that deregulation would lead to lower prices and offer customers choices. One of the principal intended effects was the economic signal of market prices, which would improve system load factor (as opposed to the perverse rate structure which existed under regulation). In the electric industry, there is no practical way of storing electricity for later use. The absence of storage results in much more supply capacity in relation to demand (and resultant low load factor) than almost any other industry. Demand is almost completely inelastic. The result is that system load factors are commonly between 50% to 60% on an annual basis.

Since electricity is considered an essential service, system authorities dictate that there be enough generation capacity such that a 15% to 20% reserve margin exists for the peak day of the year (that is, generation capacity is equal to 115% to 120% of peak day demand). This requirement is developed based on a reliability criterion, such as one service interruption (due to inadequate generation) every 10 years. The following example illustrates reserve margin. If a geographic area has a peak load of 5,000MW (i.e., the hour of the year with the highest level of demand), then there must be roughly 6,000MW of capacity installed. At the same time, the average peak load may be 4,000MW (that is, the average of the 365 daily peaks). So, by mandate, the system is in surplus by an average of 150% in this example, which is not atypical.

As a result of this market structure, for most of any given year the market is in surplus and profit margins are low. Occasionally, however, extreme load growth (either through economic growth and/or extreme weather conditions) can result in shortages during peak periods. During these periods, there have been cases of extreme price volatility. During the hot summers of 1997 and 1998, prices spiked to around $6,000 to $7,000/MWh for short periods in the mid-west. Given that the average price for a MWh is usually about $40/MWh, this represented something on the order of a 100 sigma event. Regulatory agencies have since implemented price caps at $1,000/MWh.

Price Volatility Continues

Price volatility is still a significant risk in the electric industry, notwithstanding the price caps. Under the regulated environment, serving (that is, supplying) load was relatively riskless. Firstly, price volatility was minimal. Secondly, any costs associated with serving load, as long as prudently incurred, would be recovered by the utility. In the deregulated environment, market price risk is now usually borne by companies serving the load, rather than customers. And this price risk must now be analytically modeled as well as priced into the service.

Most of the price risk can be hedged by purchasing forward blocks of energy to match anticipated sales volumes. However, another risk associated with this type of sale is volumetric.

Swing Options and Managing Volumetric Risk

Sales to end-users are referred to as "full requirements". This means that customers do not commit to purchase an exact fixed volume of energy (MWhs). The supplier agrees to provide as many MWhs as the customer needs. Consider a homeowner who uses more air conditioning in a hot summer versus a cool summer. The customer pays a fixed rate, in terms of cents/kWh (kilowatt-hour), regardless of usage or load factor. The supplier must be prepared to provide more MWhs in a warm summer (1MWh equals 1,000kWhs. In this write-up, the two terms are used interchangeably). This creates a hedging dilemma. If the supplier purchases MWhs ahead of time in anticipation of a warm summer, and the summer is actually cool, the supplier will have extra MWhs of which it will need to dispose. If the supplier hedges lightly in anticipation of a cool summer, it could be short if the summer is warm, and that could cost it dearly.

This aspect completely changes the dynamics of risk in this industry. In the financial industry, from which many principles of risk management have been borrowed, quantities of shares, bonds, options, and so forth are generally fixed, and the focus in terms of risk is price risk. In the power industry, price risk is a major concern as well. However, volumetric risk adds to the uncertainty and risk management and pricing of products and services need to reflect this risk.

Load, Price and Weather Risk Components

The nature of volumetric risk involves three key interrelated parameters: load, price, and weather. The relationship among these is such that it is almost always a cost to the load supplier. That is, these three variables are highly correlated. This represents an additional cost, and the supplier bears the risk of this cost. It is the responsibility of the supplier to estimate the expected cost, including perhaps a risk premium for its uncertainty.

As an example, assume that a supplier forecasts a load of 100MW peak load for a day in July. Based on that load forecast, the supplier purchases 100MW of on-peak supply (on-peak is usually defined as the five weekdays, covering the time period roughly from 8 a.m. through 11 p.m.). The cost of this supply is $50/MWh, and the supplier charges the retail customers $55/MWh to allow for some profit.

If the day is very warm, then most people have their air conditioners on at full level, resulting in high MWh usage or load levels. This is the first relationship. That is, load and weather tend to be highly correlated. MWh usage is a direct result of extreme weather. As demand for power increases, prices in the spot market for power also increase. This is the second relationship: market prices are correlated to load levels. Or alternatively, as demand increases, so does the price. This relationship among three variables is costly for the supplier.

Returning to the example, warm temperatures result in a higher load than forecasted (which had been 100MW). Assume the actual load is 110MW. The supplier, having only purchased 100MW ahead of time to meet the expected load, now is short 10MW, which must be purchased in the spot market. However, since demand is great spot prices are high (say $75/MWh). So, the supplier, who charged the customer $55/MWh based on a $50/MWh supply cost, is now incurring incremental costs, as the supplier must now purchase MWhs for $75/MWh which are being sold for $55/MWh.

Had that same day been cooler than normal, the opposite situation would have occurred. In that case, the actual load would have come in lower than expected (say 90MW). Lower overall demand would have resulted in lower spot prices (assume $25/MWh). Now, the supplier is in the position of being long 10MW, which it must now sell into the spot market at a loss of $25/MWh, which again is an additional cost. As the example has shown, the supplier loses in both scenarios.

These phenomena are collectively referred to as a "swing" option. It is a volumetric option, and gives the holder (the customer) the right to call on more volume (at the same fixed price) when it is economical to do so and simultaneously has the right to put volume back to the seller (at the same fixed price) again when economical. Therefore, the swing option is really two options (a call and a put). The writer of the swing option is selling both a call and a put. This is also known as a straddle.

When prices are either high or low, the supplier will financially lose. This is the definition of a short straddle. The payout function is asymmetric. There is no way for the supplier to gain. The best scenario is for prices to be at a neutral level and the supplier will neither gain nor lose. However, even in that scenario, the supplier still bears the risk that events could have been worse, and needs to maintain risk capital to cover against that contingency, which is costly.

A factor that will influence the value of the swing option is, of course, volatility; the volatility of both the load and price, as well as the correlation between the two. Higher volatilities will increase its value (or cost to the supplier), as well as high correlation between load and price. In practical terms, high load volatility means large forecast errors. Large forecast errors mean risk exposure to spot market prices. And with simultaneous (i.e., highly correlated) high market prices, this could result in higher costs than a lower volatility load and market price, with lower correlation.

Another factor that impacts the value of the swing option is the nature of exercise on the user's part. That is, does the holder of the option (the end use customer) exercise the option solely based on economics? Or is the user just concerned with its load requirements? Obviously, if the user will exercise based on economics, this option will be more costly to the writer than if the user is not completely optimizing the option.

A supplier needs to factor into its price expectations of the swing option cost (i.e., the value of the swing option). One approach would be to perform a Monte Carlo simulation, modeling the load, price, and correlation based on historically observed patterns. This approach may prove too time-consuming if pricing out many deals. In such a case, it may make sense to run the simulation for a "typical" customer and use that estimate across the board. Also, once one has enough experience writing such options, there is also the benefit of using historic costs associated with the swing option. Additionally, Monte Carlo analysis or history can also reveal worst case costs, and the supplier may elect to charge the customer some premium for bearing that risk as well.

Load Forecasting

One of the major risks in load supply is load-forecasting accuracy. As described in the above swing option example, any deviation between existing supply (which is usually based on the load forecast) and actual load is subject to risk of loss. If the load forecast is very inaccurate, chances are that the supplier will experience a higher level of swing option costs and be less profitable. Alternatively, this supplier will need to charge a higher price for the same product and be less competitive in the markets. In terms of minimizing exposure to swing option costs, as well as minimizing risk (and being more competitive), one needs the most accurate load forecast possible.

Of course any forecast is just that: a forecast. And every forecast will be wrong. However, in terms of expectations (that is, on average), an effort to produce a forecast that is as accurate as possible will on average help to minimize errors, and in the long run lead to lower costs and higher profitability. Thus, load forecasting can be considered a core skill for a corporation, and creates a competitive advantage for the firm.

There are many factors that impact electric consumption: GDP, employment levels, appliance usage, and so forth. One of the main factors that influence electric consumption, especially in the short-term, is weather. Weather impacts the load forecast in two ways: historic (actual) weather has influenced historic load data, and future weather will influence future loads. Both need to be evaluated in the development of a load forecast.

In developing a load forecast, a common approach is to develop one based on "normal" weather. Normal weather would be based on the last 10 or 20 years. While any given year's weather may be normal, warm, or cold, the advantage from a suppler perspective is that basing a supply plan using normal weather will at least minimize errors. In the long run, using a forecast based on normal weather should result in lower costs. Normal weather, by definition, will be based on an average of past weather conditions. This should minimize errors.

Weather normalizing load data involves stripping out the component of load that was caused by abnormal weather conditions. This can be accomplished through a regression analysis of historic load to weather. In terms of quantification of weather, the appropriate units would be either Cooling Degree Days (CDDs) or Heating Degree Days (HDDs). For the regression, the slope of the line is the change in load per unit of HDD or CDD change.

One can also distinguish between weekdays and weekends, as the slopes may be different. That is, load may be much more responsive to weather on a weekday than weekend. So it is important to develop a separate coefficient for these two time periods. The same can be said for seasons. For winter periods one would need to use HDDs as the weather data, and for summer periods CDDs.

Once the coefficients have been calculated, it is now possible to weather normalize the historic load data. By comparing historic degree days versus historic load, one can adjust the load to produce what the load would have been had the weather been normal. Historic, weather normalized load data can now be extrapolated to a forecast based on an assumed load growth rate.

A special issue involves customer counts. Customer counts are defined as simply the number of customers. Load growth is a function of higher customer counts as well as higher usage per customer. If customer counts are not expected to change radically, this is not so significant. However, if there is a perception that customers can switch to other suppliers, special care must be taken in evaluating the potential economic loss associated with this risk. There is also a "risk" if more customers than expected sign up for supply. This may sound counter-intuitive. Usually, more customers are good. However, more customers that sign up for service at a predetermined price at a time when such price is uneconomic (i.e., prevailing market prices have increased) will result in additional costs than expected. In the power industry, price volatility is such a significant risk that any change in volumes (increase or decrease) can result in economic loss.

The reason is based on the fact that hedges are placed at the time of deal origination. Hedges are based on the expected load forecast at that time. If a significant amount of load switches to alternate suppliers, it is not just a matter of profit foregone. The supplier has hedges, which now will have to be unwound, and a significant risk exists that market prices have decreased. Conversely, any increase in load, either through new customers or weather related, will subject the supplier to risk that market prices may have increased.

Price Forecasting/Monte Carlo Simulation

Price forecasting is an important aspect in overall risk control and pricing. However, a distinction between forward prices and forecasted prices is critical. Generally, a hedge plan is developed in which forward purchases of energy will cover most of the anticipated sales of energy. An exception would be swing risk. Anticipated price forecasts are helpful in evaluating this option. However, any static analysis understates the expected cost of this option (or any option, for that matter).

The optimal method for pricing any full requirements deal is with the use of a Monte Carlo simulation; the reason being that there are so many uncertain variables, all interacting with varying degrees of correlation, that any closed-form solution is suspect. The components of a Monte Carlo simulation could include: load variability, power price volatility, load forecast volatility (including expected growth, potential loss or gain in customers), as well as other items that may be part of the sales arrangement (which could include sale of capacity, ancillary services, congestion, etc.).

Monte Carlo analysis can help because it involves simulations based on input assumptions for the above variables. Other important data would include estimated minimum and maximum values for the inputs, as well as assumed price distributions, volatilities, and correlations to other variables. The results will include expected costs for the variables, including an expected cost for the swing option. Under multiple simulations, the model will generate a spectrum of costs, and the average value will be a reasonable indication of its expected cost.

A Monte Carlo model will also show a VaR (value at risk) scenario. If the supplier chooses a 95th percentile definition for

VaR, simply sorting each of the simulation's P&L outcomes, and directly observing the 95th percentile case, can identify this. This would be the VaR case.

The VaR is an important tool for two reasons. On the one hand, it is a gauge to measure the risk of loss on the deal, and whether this magnitude of loss is consistent with the supplier's risk profile and risk policies. A second issue is that any profit requirement for the supplier may be gauged based on the amount of risk taken in the deal. Companies will have various ways to ensure that reward is commensurate with risk taken. Knowing the VaR will help a supplier determine its profit requirement.

Another way in which Monte Carlo can be useful is by assessing company-wide risk. As stated above, a company requires profit based on incremental risk. If the load deal increases risk to the corporation, then a commensurate profit should be priced into the deal. However, if this particular load deal is negatively correlated with other company assets, then this deal may in fact decrease risk to the corporation, requiring less or no profit at all. For example, if the supplier also owns generation assets and can use this deal as a way to help lock-in profits, that can be considered mitigating overall corporate risk. This could be a factor guiding the profit decision.

Editor's Notes on Quantitative Techniques and the Utilities Industry

Econometric Modeling, Data Mining and Forecasting Accuracy

As was mentioned in the preceding chapter, an essential way to help manage risk in the utilities industry is by increasing the accuracy of electricity demand and price forecasts. When considering the forecasting issue for longer term periods of time for which supply of power for corresponding customers has been established (e.g., seasonal, annual), multivariate econometric models involving regression or neural network methods can be utilized to help enhance forecasting accuracy. These models incorporate driver/independent variables such as general economic indicators (e.g., GDP, employment) and also weather-related variables that affect the target/dependent variable of load demand. This type of modeling generally relies on quantitative and statistical techniques that incorporate the rules of economic theory in explaining the variance of electricity demand. Two such examples are depicted in Kokkelenberg and Mount (1993), who incorporated a complex system of equations in a regression model to forecast longer term trends in electricity demand, and Kudyba (1998), who illustrated the advantages neural networks provide to increase forecasting accuracy.

The topic of managing risk in the utilities industry also includes a shorter term horizon that involves the fluctuations of price and load demand that may result from changes in weather patterns over a daily, weekly or monthly basis. Over a shorter time horizon, variations in load demand can also be a function of the hourly time segments within days of the week along with the type of day (e.g., business day or weekend). Regression or neural networks once again can be effective methodologies to identify the relationships between such driver variables as temperature, humidity, dew point, time of day, cloud cover, and others, and the target variable of load and price levels. The powerful computational nature of neural net architectures may have the ability to identify important nonlinear relationships between driver variables (e.g., temperature) and load. What is needed is historical data of weather-related and corresponding target variables such as electricity demand (e.g., load). Figures 1 and 2 depict the type of detailed data that can be utilized to generate forecasting models in the utility industry.

The incorporation of such quantitative methods in the econometric and data mining spectrums help to create models that generate future forecasts given changes in input variables. These models can potentially be used by suppliers of energy to adjust their productive resources and pricing policies in the attempt to mitigate their risk and enhance their operating efficiency.

Figure 1: Daily Weather-Related Data on Demand

WeatherDate	Temp	DewPoint	Humidity	CloudCover	SunMin	Load
6/3/1998	71	62	73	5	65	1600
6/4/1998	76	59	78	7	60	1620
6/5/1998	77	64	75	12	55	1645
6/6/1998	85	60	84	14	45	1720

Figure 2: Hourly Segments of Load

Day	Trading Interval Hour End	Actual System Load
8/1/2002	1	15402
8/1/2002	2	14477
8/1/2002	3	13859
8/1/2002	4	13533
8/1/2002	5	13545
8/1/2002	6	14153
⇩	⇩	⇩
8/1/2002	14	23633
8/1/2002	15	23715
8/1/2002	16	23664
8/1/2002	17	23551
8/1/2002	18	23089
8/1/2002	19	22256
8/1/2002	20	21473
8/1/2002	21	21387
8/1/2002	22	20472
8/1/2002	23	18494
8/1/2002	24	16540

The "Hour End" variable refers to the 24-hour segments in a given day and "System Load" is demand during that period.
Data Source: ISO New England Inc. (http://www.iso-ne.com)

Closing Comments

This chapter sought to provide a clearer understanding of the dynamic nature of the utility industry and also illustrate the main factors that introduce risk to companies that supply energy to users. Quantitative methods such as regression and Monte Carlo analysis can potentially help suppliers increase forecast accuracy of expected demand and price change to better adjust their ability to reduce the variance of meeting demand in their marketplace.

Endnotes (Editor's Section)

Kokkelenberg, E. and Mount, T. (1993). "Oil Shocks and the Demand for Electricity," The Energy Journal, *14(2).*

Kudyba, S. and Diwan, R. (1998). "Are Neural Networks a Better Forecaster?" Futures Magazine, *October.*

About the Editor

 **Stephan Kudyba** (PhD) is a faculty member in the School of Management at the New Jersey Institute of Technology (USA) where he teaches graduate courses in Data Mining and Knowledge Management. He is also president and founder of Null Sigma Inc., a consulting company that concentrates on enhancing corporate operational efficiency through the utilization of Data Mining, Business Intelligence and Knowledge Management initiatives. To help enhance corporate productivity, the company focuses on a number of business applications that include marketing/advertising effectiveness, customer relationship management (CRM) and human resource management, to name a few, for organizations across industry sectors. Dr. Kudyba has also held managerial and executive positions at Citibank (New York), Dresdner Bank (New York and Frankfurt, Germany) and most recently at Cognos Corporation. He has authored the books *Data Mining and Business Intelligence: A Guide to Productivity* and *IT, Corporate Productivity and the New Economy* along with a number of magazine and journal articles that address the utilization of information technologies and management strategy to enhance corporate productivity. Dr. Kudyba regularly presents at academic conferences, corporate seminars and university symposiums on corporate productivity. He holds an MBA from Lehigh University and a PhD in Economics with a focus on the Information Economy from Rensselaer Polytechnic Institute.

About the Authors

Theodore L. Perry, PhD (American Healthways) was promoted to Vice President of Informatics in June 2002 at American Healthways Inc. Before joining American Healthways, he was Manager of Program Safeguards at CIGNA HealthCare Medicare Administration. Dr. Perry is also President of Health Research Insights, a group of health care consultants with expertise in Public Health, Epidemiology, Dentistry, Internal Medicine, Biostatistics, Psychology, Nursing and Information Technology. Dr. Perry is a member of the American Statistical Association (ASA), American Medical Informatics Association (AMIA), and the Disease Management Association of America (DMAA). He has a Doctor of Philosophy in Psychology from Vanderbilt University, a Masters of Arts in Psychology from Vanderbilt University and a Bachelor of Arts in Psychology from Clark University.

Russ Danstrom (Blue Cross Blue Shield) is Executive Director of Small Accounts Sales & Promotions for Anthem Blue Cross and Blue Shield. Russ earned his BA at the University of Richmond and his MBA from the Kenan-Flagler School of Business at the University of North Carolina, Chapel Hill.

Jeff Nicola (Blue Cross Blue Shield) is a Certified Six Sigma Black Belt and Manager of Customer Acquisition Analysis for Anthem Blue Cross and Blue Shield. He has published several anthropological archaeology articles and co-authored a business case study. Jeff earned his BA from Northwestern University, MA from the University of Virginia, and MBA from the College of William & Mary Graduate School of Business.

Jeff Hoffman (Chubb & Son, a division of Federal Insurance Company) is currently Vice President of Customer and Market Intelligence and E-Business of Chubb & Son, a division of Federal Insurance Company. He is responsible for Business Intelligence, Market Research and E-Business where he sets strategy, directs and provides oversight related to developing intelligence information from internal and external sources. In leading Chubb's Market Research team he is accountable for developing scope, managing, executing and summarizing results of qualitative and quantitative research initiatives. Jeff also directs and leads Chubb's E-Business efforts, focusing on supporting common platforms, setting standards and gathering Web visitation intelligence. Jeff received his BA in Economics from Rutgers University in 1984. He completed the Wharton School of the University of Pennsylvania Insurance Executive Development Program in September 2000.

Ákos Felsővályi (Citigroup) is currently a Vice President in the Risk Architecture Unit at Citigroup. He develops various risk assessment tools utilizing the vast amount of financial data of the Corporation. Previously, he worked in Direct Marketing at the company's credit card business, where he was mining the credit card data and constructed a range of statistical models. He holds an MS in Applied Mathematics from his native country, Hungary.

Jennifer Courant (Citigroup) is currently a Vice President of Risk Modeling in the Risk Architecture Unit at Citigroup. She develops and supports credit risk models for use in the bank's corporate lending business. She has been previously employed as a real estate economist at AEW Capital Management. She holds a BS in Economics from Saint Vincent College.

Nicholas Galletti (Con Edison Energy) is Director of Financial & Market Analysis at Con Edison Energy, a subsidiary of Consolidated Edison Inc. He gained his pricing experience by overseeing the financial evaluation of the Company's structured transactions and asset investments. Mr. Galletti is a graduate of New York University's Leonard M. Stern School of Business, where he holds a Master's Degree in Business Administration (Finance). He also has a Bachelor's Degree in Mechanical Engineering from Manhattan College.

Navin C. Sharma, PhD (Marketwell Inc.) is President of Marketwell, Inc., a consulting company which provides Data Warehousing, Database Marketing, and Data Mining services to corporations in a variety of industries. He has over twenty years of experience in Marketing Research, Modeling, Information Technology, and Systems Integration and has consulted with major firms in such sectors as Cosmetics, Banking, Brokerage, Publishing, and Travel and Leisure. Mr. Sharma has a bachelor's in Mechanical Engineering and PhD in Sociology from the University of Illinois.

David Martin (Nielsen//NetRatings) is a data analyst with the Nielsen//NetRatings Client Analytics department. The department specializes in mining online advertising and website traffic databases to help clients address complicated business questions with answers that lie outside the scope of NetRatings's syndicated data services. David spends his time writing SQL queries and macros to mine and manipulate data, and provides project costs and turnaround time estimates for clients. He holds a bachelor's degree from Harvard University and spends his free time as a competitive distance runner.

Robert Young (PHD Canada, A Subsidiary of Omnicom Group Inc.) is a founding partner of Harrison, Young, Pesonen and Newell Inc., which began operation in 1979 and has grown over the last 20 years into one of Canada's largest media management companies, currently billing over $300 million. HYPN is part of the PHD network of media companies, which, in turn, is owned by Omnicom. Rob has been responsible for HYPN's Media Planning and Media Research output which provides Media Planning services for many of Canada's largest and most sophisticated advertisers including such accounts as Unilever, Honda, Cara and Home Hardware. HYPN's Media Research services often involve providing advertising value assessments for broadcasters; providing print media evaluation for publishers; providing data mining and econometric evaluations of his client's media programs. He currently is Chair of the Board of Directors of the Print Measurement Bureau.

Vernon E. Gerety, PhD (PredictiveMetrics, Inc.) is the Senior Vice President of PredictiveMetrics, Inc. (formerly Predictive Business Decision Systems, PBDS). He is responsible for business development of custom knowledge-based solutions for new and existing clients and for the development of new products and services. Prior to joining PredictiveMetrics, Vernon spent over ten years in various management positions at AT&T, D&B, GE Capital and Advanta Business Services. Vernon was responsible for leading teams of people in setting up and integrating automated knowledge-based strategic initiatives. He earned his PhD in Economics from the University of Arizona in Tucson and his BA from California State University, Fresno.

Index

I

K

L

M

N

O

P

Q

R